The Brightness of Stars

The Brightness of Stars

Stories of Adults Who Came Through The British Care System

Lisa Cherry

Wilson King, Publishers
Banbury, Oxfordshire

The Brightness of Stars
Stories of Adults Who Came Through The British Care System

British Library Cataloguing in Publication Data.
A catalogue record for this book is available from the British Library.

Published in the UK by Wilson King Publishing
ISBN: 978-0956331090

Printed by Print on Demand Ltd, Peterborough
This book is printed on environmentally friendly paper

FSC PEFC

Photograph credits, Jenny Stewart
Cover design by Steve Shepherd
Cover Artwork: Joy Aitman

All efforts have been made to observe the legal requirements with regard to the rights of suppliers of photographic and other materials.

Disclaimer
This guide is for information purposes only and is not intended as a substitute for legal or other professional services. Readers are urged to consult a variety of sources and educate themselves fully. The information expressed herein is the opinion of the author, and is not intended to reflect upon any particular person or company. The author and publisher shall have no responsibility or liability with respect to any loss or damage caused, or alleged to be caused, by the information or application of the information contained within this guide.

"All parents damage their children.
It cannot be helped. Youth, like pristine glass,
absorbs the prints of the handler.
Some parents smudge, others crack, a few shatter
childhoods completely into jagged little pieces beyond repair."

The Five People You Meet In Heaven
Mitch Albom

THE BRIGHTNESS OF STARS

Contents

THE BRIGHTNESS OF STARS

Acknowledgements

I would like to take this opportunity to thank everyone who was not there for me, everyone who wouldn't or couldn't listen to me and everyone who failed to protect me. For it is you that I am most indebted to as you gave me the greatest gift that I have, which is that I am a person who has been on a journey that has enabled me to be deeply proud and strong and filled with an immense appreciation of all that I am.

I also need to thank all of the contributors to this book who dug deep - really deep, and often when they didn't want to - so that they too could share their stories.

A big thank you must go to all my wonderful supportive friends who are really my family, and also to the amazing online community that stretches across three continents, of which I am massively a part.

Mr Smith has become an integral part of all that I do and I intend it to be the case that he remains so.

Finally everything I do, I do for my children so that they can have the best life they can possibly have. They taught me how to be a mother; they taught me how to love.

THE BRIGHTNESS OF STARS

THE BRIGHTNESS OF STARS

Introduction

It is said that we all have a book within us and I am no exception. I sat for months, if not years, with the burning desire to write a book. I have always felt that I was a writer: an unpublished writer who found great relief upon discovering the invention of blogging. From the moment I discovered blogging I wrote about everything, absolutely everything - every pain, every joy, every misunderstood emotion.

Blogging is where this all really began and the pleasure, relief and cathartic healing that overcame me is what allowed me to believe that I could write an entire book! For a long time I have felt that I had many stories to tell: stories that would heal the wounds left over from years of therapeutic intervention, 12 step programmes and self help books galore. And ultimately, stories that would help others. I have learnt that I need to share my stories with others and I need the space to do so in a non-judgemental, supportive place. I have learnt that we will mostly benefit from telling our stories and I have learnt that I have *only* found benefit in telling my stories. And when we stand up and stand out and share our story we open up the possibility of helping another person heal too.

My first book, Soul Journey, quenched my thirst but it was barely off the printer before I threw myself into writing this book.

I wanted to write something more autobiographical, something more about what I have seen unravelling, more about what shapes us as adults and what we are left to deal with and heal and recover from. I was in care for part of my childhood and I have spent many years learning to deal with the aftermath of my experience. Gradually I have become aware of the silence of the voices of adults who were in care. We are the carriers of the quiet stories, the silent ones, the versions of life that are often untold. I wanted my voice to be heard – and I wanted to provide a space for the voices of others too. Policy makers still do not appear to ask for the views of those who have spent a lifetime dealing with the aftermath of the 'care experience'. The voice of the adult, and where life has taken them, is nowhere to be found. In fact, I found one piece of research by The Who Cares Trust[1] and little else.

More recently, however, there has been a recognition that young people in and leaving care can influence departmental policies and often sit on interview panels and contribute to debates. There are now many measuring tools in place, each year providing statistics and data about 'outcomes' for care leavers. There is also data available regarding 'things' such as money on offer, practical support and assistance and guidance on how to read your files etc. What is missing is how it 'feels' to be a child in care – and how those feelings continue to affect children long into adulthood. Through the stories in this book, I intend to shed some light on the emotional side of being in care, and I hope that this may somehow influence the reader. If you are a policy maker, consider this to be knowledge for informing and shaping good practise. If you are a practitioner or teacher, then use this book to add to your skills. If you have been in care, enjoy the connection. If you are finding out about it for the first time, enjoy being privy to knowledge that is so often hidden, unspoken of and buried.

For the purposes of clarification, when I refer to care leavers I mean young people under 24 years of age. I have heard people in their 50s refer to themselves as care leavers and that's entirely up to them. I can be labelled as many things long before I would get to care leaver and I have had a multitude of experiences in this thing called life, so it seems completely irrelevant to me to think of myself in this way. I am an adult that experienced being in care

---

[1] The Who Cares? Trust is a voice for children in care. Everything they do is designed to improve the day-to-day experience of children and young people – and their future lives. www.thewhocarestrust.org.uk

as a child/young person; I am not a professional care leaver, a professional alcoholic or a professional ex-homeless person. The past is very far away and has offered me many riches in terms of personal growth, development and tools to help others but it is not a 'place' I inhabit.

This book is a recognition that because of my background I have a unique set of experiences that can be linked directly to having been in care and I wanted to hear and give voice to others to see if they had similar tales, to make sense of what I found and also to make some of what I discovered explicit, for all to hear.

This is not a sensationalist piece of work designed to satisfy the hunger for trauma and drama that may reside within some. None of us lives in isolation, however isolated we have sometimes felt. We have children, partners and family members who may not know all of our life experiences or may be in denial, all of whom could read this book. I am respectful and sensitive to them and their interpretation of events where I need to be. This is not a warts 'n' all document of our lives. It is an exploration of events and how we can learn from them, a means by which those who work in this system can gain an insight and a knowledge into their daily practice. It is available to policy makers who make decisions every day about things they really know little of. The learning opportunity is therefore open to all; the means by which we recover from these events and make sense of them and then attempt to make our way into adult life is exposed.

It has been an interesting journey exploring the areas of my life that have presented themselves for inclusion. Sometimes my varied, often troubled, complex life almost seems like it belongs to another. Other times, it nestles in my diaphragm, clinging tightly to my solar plexus, weaving and interweaving between all my muscular fibres. I am unclear whether writing it down will make it more of a 'story' that I am detached from or whether it will bring me and my experiences closer together.

I started writing this particular piece from a ground floor room, a basic room, on a beach in Lefkada, Greece. For a week I spent my mornings sitting on a little plastic chair working on a plastic table covered in fruit and bottled water on a very shabby terrace. The trees nearby served as 'poles' to tie string to, to provide the washing with somewhere to dry. Homeless, permanently hungry cats and gorgeous geckos whizzed past me every now and again. The sea was right in front of me, with its many shades of blue all sitting next to each other – or were they on top of each other? - like a tapestry of sea, not dissimilar to the green tapestry of the English countryside. Were I inclined, I could throw a stone into the water; it is that close. It is in this moment that I acknowledge that I am exactly where I am meant to be. This place - a place where I have never been before, a place I have never even seen a picture of - is exactly the way it looked when I visualised myself writing at my laptop, being that which I have always believed myself to be: a writer.

In the visualisation of my writing place, the water was a lake, not the sea, but even that has been resolved. The sea in front of me actually looks like a lake: with mountains ahead and the mainland to the left of me, the illusion is that the land is surrounding the sea, holding the water. Things are often not as they seem. It looks like a lake but I know it is the sea. Sometimes we may know that something is one thing but it looks completely different. I know who I am, where I've been and who is missing from the tapestry of my life.

My desire for story telling through a book led me to explore so many potential issues. Who was I writing for? I concluded I was writing for me and my hope was that I would be writing for you too - but to avoid inhibiting my writing, my needs were to me first and foremost. I have heard many people say that you should write for yourself and then others may or may not read your ramblings, but to attempt to write for an audience that you haven't met yet would result in writing that was not congruent and lacked integrity, two of my most important prerequisites to doing anything.

What about privacy? In writing about our innermost emotional dealings with our experiences, do we give up our privacy? How will it feel to not have it any longer when I don't fully understand what losing it will actually mean? If I put my life in writing and then place it in the hands of whoever may wish to read it, then my privacy will be gone forever. I researched and read the few articles I could find on the subject and the different personal journeys of growth and discovery that writers have had to take due to handing over their privacy and telling their stories. As I mentioned earlier, I had started the process of telling my story through blogging, interviews and honest and open exchanges long before writing this book.

I realised that through that process I came to accept that my stories were not as useful when they were locked in an emotional world of the unknown: a place where fear could grow; a place that housed fear for a number of years; an emotional world filled with shame, remorse and aloneness. So I write today fully accepting that my privacy will be gone from within me.

What about everyone else's privacy? When I write about my life, it is my story, not that of anyone else who is mentioned. I fully appreciate and understand that we all have different perceptions of events, traumas and consequences, but this is mine and mine alone and I interpret all my experiences through the eyes of someone who wishes no harm; I will protect identities where I can.

So what is this book about? What is it for? What is its purpose?

It's not:

- a research project
- a representative sample of the 350,000 care leavers that I could have spoken to. [2]
- a collection of statistics

It is:

- a collection of previously unheard voices, observing the minutiae of each person's experience
- an exploration of some of the issues that people have had to deal with, providing information about the types of intervention that would be beneficial for the 16-24 year old age group
- an insight to further understanding

Lots of people grow up facing all sorts of challenges that are taken into adulthood but this book is about 'care' in the UK and the impact it has on children that is then carried with them through their lives. I also want to counterbalance the information out there regarding outcomes with some positive benefits that care leavers have taken from their experience.

Predominately, the statistics currently available are generally collected from 16-18 year olds to provide data about NEETs (Not in Education, Employment or Training) or are collected by organisations such as mental health services, prisons, etc. to demonstrate the population within those groups who have a care background (amongst other things). How different, I wonder, would that data be if it were collected from 30 year olds? Is it implausible to think that those early years after being in care are focused around recovery and learning survival skills to 'get you onto your feet' and that the resilience learned through childhood

---

[2] Care Leavers Association

experiences can then carry that young person into adulthood with a fierce will to succeed? It happens - regularly, it seems. But you are unlikely to find any data about it.

As a parent, can you imagine not knowing or having any information about the child you looked after - your child - after the age of 16 or 18 or 21? Put like that, it highlights the absurdity of the absence of data that could inform and underpin practice.

Through the process of gathering the stories for this book I often felt as though I was looking in the mirror as I listened to the experiences of others. For while each story is so completely different, there were many similarities about the impact of being in care and what that has given us to deal with as adults, both positive and negative.

So while this is not a piece of research, there are recurrent themes to be taken from here that can add to an understanding and a more compassionate approach towards the children that society undertakes to 'look after'.

The reports will continue to be released each year and it is vital that we have this information to 'measure' progress and provide better services. But the stories in here are not focused on the practical 'things'. This is more a journey about how it 'feels', or how it felt - the emotions, the impact, the way we can learn, grow and develop from those experiences. Not what was 'done' but how we 'felt'. If you are a practitioner, consider that element of this as a tool for change and understanding. If you are a policy maker, consider this knowledge for informing and shaping good practice. If you have been in care, enjoy the connection. If you are finding out about it for the first time, enjoy being privy to knowledge that is so often hidden, unspoken and buried.

THE BRIGHTNESS OF STARS

THE BRIGHTNESS OF STARS

Chapter One
1970 - 1980

I am more whole than I have ever been.
This book is brought to you from all of me:
the child who has been in care,
the child who has been homeless, the recovering alcoholic,
the woman with a degree in Sociology,
the woman with an endless fascination for politics and society,
the mother of teenagers, the person who worked in Social Services,
Leaving Care Teams and Social Inclusion,
the woman who has been on a self-development journey for 22 years,
the lover of chocolate and coffee.

I offer it all. I am not to be placed in a box that can be ticked. After all - and I want you to really understand and believe this - none of us are ...

This is a story about love and pain and hurt and isolation; a depth of a life, the big things and the little things. We don't live our lives in theories and philosophies, we live them through our relationships with others and where we feel we reside within those relationships. It is how we explain those relationships that enable us to tell our stories and I tell mine through the language of emotion; through the feelings that I have been left with. For it is that which I will always remember: how I felt.

My whole arrival into the world seems to me to have been surrounded by shame. I think the fact that my mother had had sex at all was too much for my gran to bear. As far as I could tell, sex was an activity endured by a married woman in return for being looked after, for being housed. I remember my gran talking about the 'red cape' that she made my mother wear to 'hide the baby' and I remember thinking, "That's me. I'm the baby. Why would you want to hide me?" Of course I only know what I have been told, the stories changing through the passage of time and the storytellers and, of course, through their own journeys of understanding. The rest of what I know is the emotional imprint left upon my soul and in my cells which have taken, and continue to take, a long journey of recovery and healing.

So it's 1969, and as I understand it, my mother had been 'dating' someone for a few months, maybe three. His name has always been a mystery but Dave and Fred have been mentioned on the various occasions that I have tried to have a conversation about who this mystery person - my father - may be. A night out in Wigan, a few drinks, a gullible and possibly sheltered and vulnerable twenty-year-old girl became a recipe for disaster. The young woman has a good night out and then pays the price forever. On this night, I am conceived.

The backdrop for my first ten years is Southport, a northern town roughly sandwiched between Manchester and Liverpool, filled with beautiful Victorian architecture and gaudy ice cream parlours selling Knickerbocker Glories, the ultimate dessert of the 1970s seaside resort.

Lord Street carries the air of a shopping street to savour, with its Victorian shopping arcades, its closeness to the seafront and the large buildings competing for appreciation. I doubt it was a very forward thinking town in 1969 and being a teenager here may well have been quite stifling, especially knowing that in other parts of the country there was a revolution going on, a complete shift into another generation and alleged sexual freedoms. The North West of England was undoubtedly still not quite ready to deal with diversity, women's liberation and, of course, birth outside marriage.

I seem to remember my gran telling me that one day 'he' (the man I believe to be my dad) came to our house in Zetland Street. It was a three bedroom semi-detached Victorian house; a lovely house with a garden that, to my child's eye, seemingly went on forever. He was told at the door that I had been aborted, terminated, removed - whatever terminology that you find comfortable. My French granny had told me this in her incredibly clumsy way. She was often very emotionally clumsy and had a complete lack of emotional awareness that knew no bounds. She was always deeply unaware of the impact of her words and that, coupled with English being her second language, led to many a harsh word being spoken.

Emotional comprehension and articulation just wasn't in her communication, not really in her generation, so translating a feeling was always going to lead to the strangest and most insensitive of exchanges. I was always uncomfortable about the fact that I knew this piece of information, this knowledge of hiding me, aborting me, removing me, the very nature of such a discussion serving to give out a whole multitude of messages. Not being wanted and the stories that surrounded this truth created self-loathing that I had to crawl my way out of. I would have been about 12, maybe 13, when I found out about the abortion conversation. Even then I was very aware that this was knowledge that I really ought not to have and that I may hold on to forever, and indeed I have.

I don't believe that knowledge like this is a good thing for a child, for a teenager or for a woman, but it is information that I have nonetheless, and in the emptiness of the knowledge available to me, I attempt gratitude. What I have taken from this, and what has sat in my 'emotional database', is that someone else removed my right to know my father. Not only would it be logistically a piece of magic for me to find him, but he will never search for me as he does not know I am here, and my goodness, did I spend my teenage years shouting I AM HERE!

When people first learn of this aspect of my history, I am often asked, "Have you tried to find him?", "Do you want to find him?" or "Are you upset about it?" I have had intense periods of searching, intense periods of anger and intensely overwhelming emotions of loss. The unfaltering sensation of loss and abandonment has tapped me on the shoulder throughout my entire life. I understand now that there have been endless scenarios where I have created loss and abandonment for myself to ensure repetition and certainty and some sort of strange familiarity, yet not knowing why and not knowing how to attract something else.

So here I was, the unwanted, born into one of the remaining homes for unmarried mothers after my gran had gone to the church for guidance – because in 1969 that was where you went for guidance. The shame must have wrapped itself around everyone like a blanket and stayed there as if we were in a permanent winter. It seems that there was some debate as to whether I would remain with my mother and I spent the first few weeks of my life in foster care while decisions were made.

The indulgence of retrospect and reflection has cursed me from time to time as I have imagined what life might have been like if I had been adopted rather than returned to the house with my mother and my gran. Where those who were adopted think about what their lives may have been like if they'd stayed with their birth mother, mine was the other way round. Two sides of the same coin; two aspects of the same shadow.

My belief is that this early two-week separation caused an irreparable amount of damage to our relationship. As a mother myself, I cannot imagine how I would have managed that. The biological urge to look after and protect and feed your baby is so powerful I think I could have killed a person who tried to take my baby from me.

However, I do think it's possible that the lost bonding between my mother and I could have been repaired through a positive trusting relationship, but our lack of emotional and physical connection and mutual understanding and what I perceive as her difficulties with mothering in general meant that we never recovered, and this has stayed with us to date.

For the most part, 70s Britain was not a place of emotional exploration, personal development and healing. The parents of the generation who were at this time becoming parents had been through a war and the very nature of the horror of all that war entailed meant that many conversations were just not had.

With regards to parenting, this was a time when crying babies were put to the bottom of the garden in their prams to 'have a little sleep' and gripe water still had 3.6% alcohol in it. Parenting, it seems to me, sat in a cradle of "I know you can feel it, but let's pretend you can't."

Having said that, my gran was a strong, mothering and capable woman who instilled a sense of female strength and a 'get on with it' attitude that was peppered with hugs and kisses. She was a great cook and seamstress and held her head high even when it pained her to do so. Living in those times without a husband - he had died less than a decade into their marriage - and without hope of finding any kind of replacement, learning how to put a fuse in a plug was on the menu along with how to make a good roux for a cheese sauce. For my first ten years, within this strange triangle of women, Gran was the mother, I was the daughter and my mother was more like an older sister.

THE BRIGHTNESS OF STARS

The Soundtrack

Tie a Yellow Ribbon – Tony Orlando and Dawn

(I Put my Blue) Jeans On – David Dundas

Mamma Mia – Abba

Under the Moon of Love – Showaddywaddy

Bye Bye Baby - Bay City Rollers

The Headlines

Miners' strikes

The Winter of Discontent

Elvis Presley dies

Thatcher Thatcher Milk Snatcher

The IRA

The TV

Coronation Street

Charlie's Angels

Doctor Who

Generation Game

Jim'll Fix It (the irony is not to be lost on the reader)

THE BRIGHTNESS OF STARS

Remembered Moments

Being Collected from Nursery

It's sometime in the early 1970s when I first became aware that I was supposed to have a dad. I was at nursery or primary school, I can't remember which, and my uncle, my mother's brother, was visiting once and came to collect me. My uncle has always remained in my life and while there have been difficult periods of time, our relationship has continued to be a constant and I have always valued it. In my younger days I naturally felt abandoned by him too. Why didn't he come and rescue me? Why did he let me go into care? Why did he not do something?

I remember the conversation on that walk home with him as if it were yesterday. The content of the conversation is vivid; the date isn't. Somebody – another child - said to me, "Is that your dad?" "No, silly," I replied, "he's my uncle!" The words were spoken out of the mouth of a babe as if it were far more 'normal' to have an uncle collecting you from school than a father. This triggered some internal questioning: why don't I have a dad?

It must have been around this time that I asked my mother this question, to which she replied: "He was killed ... in a plane crash." "Oh," I said. So my dad was dead. I didn't need to concern myself with the minutiae of his lack of presence because he had died while I was playing with my Sindy doll and nobody had thought to mention it before.

It was many years later, through a violent row with my mother in my screaming adolescence, that I was informed that this was an untruth. Another piece of puzzling information: it's deemed ok to say that he's dead but not to tell me what his name is ... Yet another conundrum that plagued me for many years and that I was unable to resolve.

THE BRIGHTNESS OF STARS

Chapter Two
1980 - 1983

In 1980, everything changed. I honestly believe that my gran and my mother did the best they could with the information they had at the time. I had gone to all sorts of extracurricular activities before it was popular to do so and deemed by society as a pre-requisite to 'good' parenting. Money was tight but it was found to give me dance classes, piano lessons and the Brownies. In this regard I was privileged, I suppose, but the emotional 'neglect' and bed of lies and secrecy around just about anything that might cause either one of them to 'feel an emotion' was starting to take its toll on my own development.

My need for intellectual, emotional and physical stimulation was beyond challenging, especially for my mother. The gap between what I needed and what she could provide was too big a bridge to cross. I believe I was neglected in this way but I do not say that with any blame attached to it. When we have children we have to deal with what they bring us but there was no acceptance back then of me, just as I came, as an individual with my own wishes, wants, hope and desires and because that was not shown to me, I became unable to show that to my mother. As much as she couldn't accept me she taught me, by default, not to accept her – I was unacceptable and so was she. This dynamic has plagued our relationship for decades.

This complex interplay of a triangle-shaped dynamic that lacked honesty and authenticity, along with the underpinning of non-acceptance of who we all were and how that had been manifested through this 'unwanted pregnancy', meant that by the age of 10 I was already a complex and misunderstood little girl. My emotional needs had not really been met and I had grown up in an environment filled with shame and secrets and lies. My social skills were a little odd, reflecting my home environment, and I had few friends. Saying all of that, it's possible that I would not have become such a damaged teenager had my circumstances not been about to change. It's just another reflection among the many about what might or might not have been. Who knows? Life throws so many things at us, other people create situations for us, and we learn to live with the fact that we will never know any outcome other than the one we experience.

As an adult, I can choose how I view the world. I can reframe everything if I want to and I can understand that all of the experiences I had, made me who I am today. If I so wish, I can be deeply grateful to my mother and my gran for their flaws, and also to the father who arrived that day at the front door in Zetland Street and failed to check if I really was 'aborted' - and so it goes on. But I cannot do that as a child, as a dependent, as a vulnerable human being.

For my mother, the inevitable search for a suitable mate was ongoing. It's a search I can understand as a woman and as a mother but it made little sense to me as a child. I think they met through an advert. I'm not sure of the details and I have never asked. The marriage only lasted a few months, maybe a year, yet I have some of my most vivid memories from that time - actual memories and emotional imprints of feelings felt and fear created. I think they dated for about a year before they got married though I don't recall them seeing each other that many times. In our beautiful seaside town Southport, people had a 'baath'; he lived with his two daughters on a road to nowhere in a small town in Northamptonshire that I came to loathe, where the people had a 'barth'.

I particularly remember one of these visits. The incident is not a new memory; that is, I have recalled it many times over the years, examining it over and over, searching for information in a plea to make sense of it. I would have been about nine years old and my mother was almost crying, saying she couldn't carry her suitcase any longer as it was hurting her hands. We were changing trains at Rugby on our way to the place of 'barth' - or on our way back, I don't recall. We had to walk over a footbridge to get to the right platform and I took responsibility, both emotionally and physically, for my mother's hurting hands and her suitcase. I carried the suitcase. I don't know how long I carried the case for; it may not have been long at all. But nevertheless, I was the adult carrying the heavy suitcase, an analogy I can safely use about behaviour through my teenage years and a good part of my adulthood. I am the adult. I am alone. I don't need you. I don't need anyone. I can manage, thank you very much. The impact that had on my relationships was an obvious one.

It's strange how some memories are new ones, wandering around our thinking space until we are shocked by their appearance; and then there are other memories, ones we have visited so many times. And then there are the memories that are buried so deep that even a song, a smell or a photograph won't bring them to the fore. Yet we know 'they're there somewhere, trapped in our emotional imprint.

I have spent time thinking about this in my adult life. This scene of a 9-year-old girl clutching onto a suitcase that must have been nearly as big as her features in my memory bank with such clarity. It has helped me to understand my inability to be looked after in my relationships (until I was confronted with this in my marriage), my over-developed sense of responsibility to just about everyone and a tendency to want to make sure everyone else is alright before myself. I have worked through a lot of this, through understanding it and relearning new responses and behaviours, but my early adulthood was plagued with it all.

It is within this context that the absence of a father has felt so pronounced and it is in this place that I have craved being looked after and taken care of in a healthy way, in that way that a father does.

The short marriage of my mother and the man from the advert was a disaster, lasting less than a year. It was fuelled by poor communication, anger, hurt and completely mismanaged expectations. I cannot speak for the adults; I can only surmise with adult eyes, observing through the memories of a child. But I suspect that he needed a mother for his children and my mother needed a husband. The three children, thrown together in this unlikely family, were not consulted or spoken to, or listened to. It was 1980 and emotional literacy, living consciously and listening to children were not part of popular culture. Psychologies magazine was yet to be on the shelves and I believe that it is in this setting that I felt the most emotionally neglected.

This period of time was a huge turning point for me. I felt so badly the loss of my gran, who had mothered me for ten years and remained in Southport. If I had felt as though I was different to everyone else through living with two women, one of whom was French, I certainly felt different in this place. All of a sudden, I had a dad and two sisters, Sharon and Sarah - more children experiencing more outcomes from the strange decisions taken by the adults in their lives. I was now in a step family, a completely new family with their own way of living and expectations and set of norms and values. I felt completely alone and isolated and abandoned and misunderstood and yet no one ever spoke to me about how I was feeling. Nobody said a word.

New School – September 1981

I bumbled my way through the final year of primary school in this new town in the depths of Northamptonshire with the words "Why can't you just fit in?" ringing through my ears; it was my mother's favourite sentence for a number of years. This was quickly followed by my entry into secondary school. My first secondary school was an all-girls' school and I was in the top set for most subjects; academically bright yet emotionally distressed, I was sharing my space with the children who lived in nice houses, with mums and dads and perceived harmony. It was here that I learnt the art of fantasising about other people's lives. In my little fantasy world they were all loved and cared for and listened to and understood, and being a child, I just felt jealous, painfully jealous.

My behaviour deteriorated pretty quickly. I was angry and destructive and was screaming externally and internally for someone to help me and listen to what was happening for me. Drinking and drugging commenced and my inner turmoil spilled out into just about any room I entered. At school things were so bad that I spent most of my lessons in the music room on my own and I knew that the other children were told, "If you don't behave, you'll end up like Lisa Cherry" – yes, you'll end up abandoned, lost and in the music room too!

My early teenage years felt cruel and lonely. I look at my own children and their sense of innocence and fun and discovery and belonging, and it is almost the antithesis of my own experience. I was plagued by all the usual teenage angst alongside the imbalance and instability that sits on top of living in a volatile home. The arguments between my mother and I were shocking, sometimes physical and always loudly verbal.

The manifestation of the previous 12 or so years of silenced emotion and unspoken truths exploded from within me like a tornado. This was the beginning of all that was destructive and it arrived without warning, horrifying those around me. Every piece of self-loathing behaviour stood up and made itself known. This burst of loud expression, coupled with my social ineptitude, meant that my friendships were complicated and I learnt quickly how to ensure alienation and rejection. I went from being described as incredibly "bright and promising" to "Lisa will never make much of herself". But the tragedy was that I had far bigger problems to deal with than that!

The discovery of my sexuality, which is daunting enough for any teenager, left me in undesirable and risky situations as I searched for someone to look after me and to protect me from myself.

As an adult, with many years on a healing journey under my belt alongside years working extensively with young people in equal and further distress than I experienced myself, I understand this behaviour all too well. In my search for that place of approval, of belonging, of acceptance and for someone to take care of me, I found myself in many a dark place.

Abusers, paedophiles, child traffickers, drug dealers; they know exactly where to look and what 'qualities' a child has to have in order to be 'groomed'. I am convinced today that I escaped so much because I screamed so loudly and was usually a liability to the most sophisticated abuser. I was vulnerable, oh yes, but in a loud, angry way which served me as a great protection. I have worked with many other young people, male and female, who were less fortunate and there continues to be a lucrative market in the use of vulnerable, lost children, whether they are 'in care' or not. [3]

Here is a brief overview of Acts in place to protect children and how inquiries have led to changes in legislation - and yet there is

---

[3] In May 2012, there was the conviction of nine men in Manchester who were found guilty of plying girls as young as 13 years old with alcohol and drugs prior to sexually abusing them. A mix of 'abandoned' girls, one was a Looked-After Child and the others were described of as 'from broken homes'. In other words, they were easy to identify, were not attending school and were beyond parental control.

still a mountain to climb when protecting vulnerable children and young people.

The Children and Young Persons Act 1933: one of the older pieces of child protection

legislation. It includes the list of offences against children which continue to be referred to as Schedule One offences

The Children Act 1989: This forms the basis for the current child protection system.

At the time, it was hailed as "the most comprehensive and far-reaching reform of child law which has come before Parliament in living memory" by the then Lord Chancellor Lord Mackay of Clashfern.

The United Nations Convention on the Rights of the Child 1989: ratified by the UK on 16 December 1991.

The Human Rights Act 1998: This isn't specifically about the rights of children but they are covered by this as they have rights as humans in the eyes of the law.

Children's Commissioner for Wales Act 2001: created the first children's commissioner post in the UK. The principal aim of the Commissioner is to safeguard and promote the rights and welfare of children. Subsequent legislation created a children's commissioner for Northern Ireland (The Commissioner for Children and Young People (NI) Order 2003), Scotland (Commissioner for Children and Young People (Scotland) Act 2003) and England (sections 1-9 of the Children Act 2004). The English Commissioner is unique in the UK in not having the remit to promote children's rights.

The Education Act 2002: this specifies the requirement for school governing bodies, LEAs (which we no longer have) and FE institutions to safeguard and promote the welfare of children.

Section 120 of the Adoption and Children Act 2002: amends the Children Act 1989 by

expanding the definition of 'harm' to include witnessing domestic violence.

Children Act 2004: Following the death of eight-year-old Victoria Climbié in 2000, the government asked Lord Laming to conduct an inquiry to help decide whether it needed to introduce new legislation and guidance to improve the child protection system in England. The government's response to the **Victoria Climbié Inquiry** report (Laming, 2003) was the Keeping Children Safe report (DfES, 2003) and the Every Child Matters green paper (DfES, 2003), which in turn led to the Children Act 2004.

Although much of this legislation still applies, the election of a Conservative/Liberal Democrat coalition government in May 2010 has led to a shift in thinking on child protection, and a number of changes in approach are currently under discussion.

The Children and Adoption Act 2006: gives courts more flexible powers to facilitate child

contact and enforce contact orders when separated parents are in dispute.

The Children and Young Persons Act 2008: legislates for the recommendations in the Care Matters white paper (DfES, 2007) to provide high quality care and services for children in care. It covers England and Wales (in part) and also places a duty on registrars to notify the Local Safeguarding Children Board of all child deaths. The Borders, Citizenship and Immigration Act 2009 places a duty on the UK Border Agency to safeguard and promote children's welfare (section 55), bringing them in line with other public bodies that have contact with children. The Apprenticeships, Skills, Children and Learning Act 2009 legislates for there to be two lay members from the local community sitting on each Local Safeguarding Children Board. The coalition government has since repealed some of the other provisions in this Act, including the requirement to draw up Children and Young People's Plans, and has withdrawn related statutory children's trust guidance.

The Education Act 2011 makes changes to provisions on school discipline and will place restrictions on the public reporting of allegations made against teachers.

The Sexual Offences Act 2003 was introduced to update the legislation relating to offences against children. It includes the offences of grooming, abuse of position of trust and trafficking, and covers offences committed by UK citizens whilst abroad.

The Female Genital Mutilation Act 2003 extends the existing legislation criminalising female genital mutilation in the UK by making it an offence for UK nationals or permanent UK residents to take a girl abroad, or to help others to take a girl abroad, to carry out female genital mutilation, even in countries where the practice is legal.

The Domestic Violence, Crime and Victims Act 2004: closes a legal loophole (whereby defendants in murder and manslaughter cases could escape conviction by claiming each other had killed the child) by creating a new offence of causing or allowing the death of a child or vulnerable adult. The offence establishes a new criminal responsibility for members of a household where they know that a child or vulnerable adult is at significant risk of serious harm.

The Domestic Violence, Crime and Victims (Amendment) Act 2012: extends the 2004 offence to include "causing or allowing a child or vulnerable adult to suffer serious physical harm". The amendment will come into force on a date to be announced by Statutory Instrument.

The Protection of Freedoms Act was passed on 1 May 2012. Following the 2002 murders of ten-year-olds Jessica Chapman and Holly Wells, the Bichard Inquiry (Bichard, 2004) examined vetting procedures. The government's response was the Safeguarding Vulnerable Groups Act 2006, which established a new centralised vetting and barring scheme for people working with children. Following a 2011 review of this scheme, the Protection of Freedoms Act was passed on 1 May 2012. Once commenced, the Act will see the replacement of the vetting and barring scheme with a new, scaled back disclosure and barring service which will focus only on roles working most closely with vulnerable groups.

Since the NSPCC was founded in 1884, it has played a key role in influencing and drafting legislation to protect children. [4]

The history of protecting children is relatively new and *how* we do it is a continuing debate between politicians, policy makers and media representation, often on the back of death and public outrage.

*

Real change comes when all professionals and carers in children's lives are given the emotional intelligence training to understand how to be emotionally available and connected to the young people in their care. They also need the time and space to deliver their services effectively alongside the opportunity to explore their own personal development, thus enabling them to treat children as individuals rather than trying to fit people into categories and boxes where none exist.

---

[4] This information regarding Child Protection Legislation was taken from the NSPCC website where they provide an up to date factsheet. It was correct as at May 2012. For a more detailed look at Legislation, you can go to www.nspcc.org.uk or www.legislation.gov.uk

Until that is at the heart of practice, the level of 'care', protection and attention children receive will remain a lottery dependent on the practitioner as opposed to the service itself. Everyone I spoke to had examples and experiences that reflected prejudice and social exclusion.

*

THE BRIGHTNESS OF STARS

The Soundtrack

Ant Music – Adam and the Ants

Just Can't Get Enough - Depeche Mode

One in Ten – UB40

Going Underground – The Jam

Ain't What You Do – Fun Boy Three and Bananarama

The Headlines

Royal Wedding

Yorkshire Ripper

The Falklands

John Lennon is assassinated

The TV

Dallas

Kenny Everett

Grange Hill

Private Benjamin

The A Team

THE BRIGHTNESS OF STARS

Remembered Moments

The Glass Door 1978

I'm coming home from Brownies I think and I've been dropped off outside or collected and brought home, I can't recall. It must be cold and it's definitely dark and I just want to get inside. It might even have been raining. We had a porch on our semi-detached house in Zetland Street, a posh porch, that my Gran had had specially built with a lovely half glass door. As I ran up to the house from the car that dropped me off I used the palm of my hand to push the door open as I thought it was just pulled too, but it was locked shut and my hand went straight through the glass.

There was blood everywhere. I remember my Gran and my Mother being very angry as I had broken the glass. The bandaging of my wrist was done with an angry fierce pulling and pushing and huffing and puffing. I didn't mean it, really I didn't, I'm sorry, I'm hurting. For whatever reason, it seemed to me, the glass door was far more important. The scar on my wrist is just barely visible, but remains with me; as with all scars.

*

THE BRIGHTNESS OF STARS

Chapter Three
1983

It's August 1983 and I am about to enter a system, a system that will protect me and give me and my mother much needed time apart. We had no family meetings, no discussions, no therapy, no group work. I don't remember any intervention or support offered to help my mother be a mother or help me with my emotional turmoil. No. I just remember being asked if I wanted to go and stay with another family for a few months so we could have a break.

All that happened in that first six months was that my teenage anger became firmly rooted, leaving me with no desire to speak to my mother again. Prior to leaving the rows had become more violent and nothing would have changed as no work was ever done to try and change anything. I suspect this is one of the reasons why I believe I have to hold Social Services accountable to some degree. I arrived in care with all of these difficult unanswered questions fuelled by emotional starvation and the system did not help me, try and improve things, make anything better, help me heal and grow and thrive. No. It gave the experience of 'care' in the 1980s, which was swiftly followed by the inevitable bout of homelessness and all of the risks and damage and pain that accompanied the whole experience. I couldn't help feeling that it was somehow all a bit of an accident: a series of events where no one tried to intervene - events that I should never have taken part in.

I have never seen my files, so I will never know whether my recollection is correct. I have never had the desire to read emotionless statements and perceptions from the myriad of different social workers I had during my four year 'care' experience.

THE BRIGHTNESS OF STARS

But I remember that day, the day I became a child 'in care'. I'm 13 years old and it was a stifling hot day in August 1983 and the social worker is collecting me from the flat my mother and I live in. I think the person was a woman but I can't remember. They are there to take me to my foster parents for six months – a temporary placement giving my mother and me some space, apparently. I remember very little about how this situation even came about. How do Social Services even know about me? If it had been known what being in care was going to do to me and what harsh experiences it would give me, would whoever alerted Social Services have started this road of destruction for me?

*

Who are Children In Care?

'Looked-after children' here means all children and young people who are looked after by a local authority in accordance with the Children Act 1989. It does not include those children and young people who are:

- in respite care;
- disabled and in residential provision where parental responsibility does not lie with the local authority;
- living with people other than their parents, but not under the supervision of social services;

  on remand in, or sentenced to, local authority secure units - as opposed to welfare cases. [SEU, 2003]

Statistics – Who's In Care?

There were 65,520 looked-after children at 31 March 2011, an increase of 2 per cent from 2010 and an increase of 9 per cent since 2007. [Taken from The Department of Education] [5]

- Over the course of a year, around 90,000 children will spend some time in care [Every Child Matters website, 2008]

- Of these, 73% were looked after in foster placements, 10% in secure units, children's homes and hostels, 7% with parents, 4% placed for adoption, and 5% in 'other' care (including residential schools, lodgings and other residential settings) [DCSF, 2009]

- In England in 2006, c12% of children and young people in foster placements were in kinship care, i.e. fostered by family members or friends [The Fostering Network, 2006]

- Over half of children in care (62%) are aged over 10 [DfES, 2006]

- The largest category of need for looked-after children was 'abuse or neglect', with an estimated 37,100 (61% of the total) being in this category. The second largest category was 'family dysfunction' (6,800 children, 11%) [DCSF, 2008]

- Just 2% are in care because of 'socially unacceptable behaviour' [DCSF, 2008]

- 1 in 4 children in care lives outside their 'home' local authority [SEU, 2003]

- 45,920 (78%) of the looked-after children were white; 5,000 (8%) were mixed race; 4,500 (8%) were black; and 2,800 (5%) were Asian. [DCSF, 2008]

---

[5] http://www.education.gov.uk/rsgateway/DB/SFR/s001026/sfr21-2011.pdf

- Boys, children from some ethnic minority groups, disabled children and those from lower socioeconomic groups are over-represented in care [SEU, 2003]

- Most unaccompanied asylum-seeker children aged under 16 are taken into care on arrival, and now represent about 6% of all children in care [SEU, 2003; DCSF, 2009]

- Overall, for those children who started to be looked after during the year the main reason why they were provided with a service is because of abuse or neglect (54 per cent). This percentage has increased each year since 2008 when 48 per cent of children were provided with a service for this reason.

*

Have things changed, I wonder? I think it unlikely that I would end up in care in the current climate and I know that a lot more preventative work goes on today than it ever did back in the 1980s. It's hard for me not to wonder what might have happened to me had I not been steered into that place.

There has been enough research to show that being in care can lead to all sorts of entries into other systems such as the mental health system and the prison system, for example, and that homelessness, teenage pregnancy and a lack of education are areas of concern and have a high proportion of those with a care background contained in their statistics. Lest we forget that beyond each one of those numbers is a person.

Research on the outcomes for children and young people who have been in care has been around for over 20 years. The latest statistics that I could find tell the same story that I was reading for my dissertation[6] back in 1994:

According to the latest DCSF figures [DCSF, April 2009]:

- In school year 11, in 2007-08, 66% of children looked after continuously for at least 12 months obtained at least one GCSE or GNVQ compared with 99% of all school children who gained any qualification.

- Also in 2007-08, 14% of children looked after continuously for at least 12 months obtained at least 5 GCSEs or GNVQs at grades A* to C. This compares with 65% of all school children in year 11 who gained 5 or more grades A*-C at GCSE or equivalent.

In addition:

- Children in care have poor results in Key Stage tests at ages 7, 11 and 14 [quoted in SEU, 2003]. For example, at Key Stage 1, c57% of looked-after seven-year-olds achieved at least level 2 in reading in 2008, compared with 84% of all children; at KS2, 46% of looked-after 11-year-olds achieved level 4 in English, compared with 81% of all children; and in KS3 maths, 33% of looked-after young people achieved level 5, compared to 77% of all children [DCSF, quoted in TES 5 June 2009]

- Just 6% go on to higher education [DfES, 2006]

Other impacts on future life

- In 2006, 30% of care leavers aged 19 were not in

---

[6] I wrote my dissertation on care leavers: how the system actively prevents the creation of support networks for young people entering into adult life and how this impacts upon them and their feelings of isolation.

education, employment or training (NEET) [Who Cares? Trust, 2008]

- Approximately 77,000 young people under the age of 16 run away overnight. Nearly half of young people in care have run away at some point in their lives - however, many of these young people had begun running away before they entered care [SEU, 2002].

- Between a quarter and a third of rough sleepers have been looked after by local authorities as children [SEU, 2003]

- Children who have been in care are two and a half times more likely to become teenage parents [SEU, 2003]

- Young people who have been in care are disproportionately likely to end up in prison (26% of prisoners have been in care as children, compared with just 2% of the total population) [SEU, 2003]

- Care leavers "are likely to suffer multiple disadvantages, being significantly more likely than the rest of the population to have no qualifications, to become unemployed, to be in prison, to have children whilst still a teenager, to become homeless, and to be living in poverty." [Action on Aftercare Consortium, 1996, quoted in Shaw, n.d.] [7]

*

I'm cursing and swearing and throwing all of my clothes into a bag. I empty my mother's piggy bank to buy cigarettes and I venomously shout around the flat that we shared together with

---

[7] Taken from the Social Exclusion Unit which was set up in 1997 by the government in an attempt to improve and reduce social exclusion through joined-up working.

an anger that can only be borne out of sheer frustration, disappointment and hurt. She has failed in her ability to mother me and I have failed in my ability to be mothered by her. I am out of control. I smoke, I drink endless Woodpecker Cider that I occasionally mix with spirits to ensure complete collapse, I like marijuana, I am just about to be excluded from my first school, I shoplift endlessly, my best friend has disappeared. I like Terry Hall, John Lennon, Sting and UB40. I eat rubbish, I say fuck a lot and I want to be loved. I want someone to hold me and stop this insanity that I am embarking upon. I am just a child.

*

I had many social workers so it would be impossible to recall the names of more than a couple. One was a man who I liked and he gave me his cigarettes to smoke; a winner for any smoking teenager wanting to feel heard and vaguely important. Smoking was a real tool for me to be angry and for social workers to 'befriend' me. I recognised the latter and exploited it to the max!

The other one I remember was a woman called Eunice who was allocated to me (or was I allocated to her?) for a good while during the time I was around 15 or 16 years old. She had a very cuddly appearance and drove a nice car and I always felt that she liked me more than she was meant to. I remember that feeling a lot. It was a feeling that people wanted to help or assist or 'like' me but that it wasn't allowed or appropriate or indeed relevant, for the reality is that I belonged to no one and was not the responsibility of another soul really. When that initially penetrated through the core of my being and the ability to articulate it made it real, it was a realisation that I carried as a ton of weight like a sack of stones.

The beauty of a sack of stones is that I learned to take the stones out one by one, put the bag down, throw it away. It is mine but I really don't have to carry it.

THE BRIGHTNESS OF STARS

So with regard to who collected me, I really can't recall what their name was or what they said. I was told that I was going to stay with foster parents for a break. What that actually meant was never clear and it all felt like a bit of a surprise. What sort of a family would they be? How would they live? No mention was made of what food they ate, what conversations they would have, what my room might be like; I just seem to remember arriving at a house.

It turned out to be a three bed 1930s, semi, the two double beds and a single type of house. There was a very nice car in the drive and I seemed to be meeting a 'family'. There was a mum, a dad and one, two, three children under five. Yuk! I could never quite fathom why they might want an angry teenager in the house with a workload like that but I suspect they were misguided and possibly thought I might be helpful around the home and the children.

Useful tip ... Teenagers are not helpful. Teenagers are not something that you have around the house through choice. I've never heard anyone say, "Shall we invite some teenagers round for dinner, darling, for some stimulating conversation and helpfulness?" No. And angry dysfunctional teenagers are even less helpful. This particular breed of adolescent wants to destroy everything in a sort of emotional 'quantative easing' to reduce the sensation of pain. Did nobody mention that in the training manual for foster carers?

These poor people must have been as shocked as I was at my arrival into their already busy and chaotic family home.

I don't have many memories of this six month union apart from collecting more knowledge that informed me that I was different, that I didn't 'fit in' and that I ought to be rejected back into the hands of the nameless social workers who would be able to offer another place of containment until I could be forgotten after the age of 16. I wonder, though, how many of us would be able to live in any family plucked at random and just happen to eat like they do, have sleeping patterns like they do and share their life values? I mean really, how many? It's a tall order, isn't it? Especially for a child that has been on the kind of journey that got them there in the first place.

They were, to all intents and purposes, a hardworking, middle class family trying to make a good life for their children. Every night we had a lovely big dinner with roast potatoes and vegetables and my washing was done.

The dad, Phil, worked in Sales I think, and the nice car in the drive that I had clocked upon arrival turned out to be a top of the range Austin Maestro which, at the time, was akin to something that might be used for space travel. I had never seen anything like it. It was dark blue, had lots of buttons and a dashboard like a fruit machine. It would look like the oldest car ever now, but back then it was impressive. He provided for his family and worked hard and it was, I would say, my first real experience of what having a man in the house might look like when it was a happy family - and I yearned for it. I had never lived with it before, only glimpsing it through school friends' doorways or through listening in on conversations about how people lived.

My lack of actual knowledge, coupled with the curiosity of a teenager about how everyone else lives, started the process of feeding the fantasy that I had created about families. Namely that they are wonderful, functional loving environments where you are loved and all your needs are met forever and ever - and I didn't have one, and I wanted one!! Of course my adult eyes soon started to see the world as it actually was rather than how I wanted it to be. The fantasy barely persisted past a short burst of sighs around Christmas time as I watched the fantasy world that the media portrayed through its marketing material.

THE BRIGHTNESS OF STARS

During my stay, my behaviour became more and more erratic as my ability to express myself was a voice left unheard. Without the skills of the adults around me to help me translate what I was feeling into something articulated and therefore manageable, the spiral into self-destruction took a firm hold. Rejection came quickly and easily and the next foster home awaited me.

*

THE BRIGHTNESS OF STARS

THE BRIGHTNESS OF STARS

The Soundtrack

Red Red Wine – UB40

Billie Jean – Michael Jackson

I Hear a Symphony – Diana Ross and the Supremes

Do They Know It's Christmas – Band Aid

True – Spandau Ballet

The Headlines

Tommy Cooper dies

Strike action in the coal mining industry

Prince William born

Unemployment is over 3 million

Neil Kinnock becomes Leader of The Labour Party

The TV

Torvill and Dean performing Bolero

Happy Days

Knight Rider

Sons and Daughters

Brookside

THE BRIGHTNESS OF STARS

Remembered Moments

Arriving In The Car

I'm working as a residential social worker. It's the early 1990s and I'm studying for a degree and supporting myself by being back in the very places I couldn't wait to leave: children's homes.

We have a new boy coming this morning and he's just arrived. He looks very apprehensive; he appears a little scared and he is clutching his suitcase as if it were a shield that will protect him from whatever is going to happen next. Children in care only ever seem to arrive with one bag, two at the most. I always wondered where all their things were. Mine were in my gran's loft for years.

As I look at his face I am instantly catapulted back to the very situation I had been in. I'm in the social worker's car, just like he is. I have no idea what to expect, what awaits me or even where I am going. My eyes well up as I look at him and then I quickly push down this unexpected surge of emotion and remember that I am not that child.

I am an adult now and I make the decision there and then to never look at a young person or child in care as in any way connected to me and my experience. I need to be strong, to try and forget about it. Besides, I don't really want anyone that I work with to know that I too had a life before this day, that I too have been a child in care, sitting in the car waiting to go to the next home.

*

THE BRIGHTNESS OF STARS

Chapter Four
1984 - 1985

It's February and I'm on the move. So soon. Only six months after arriving at my first foster placement, I am in the car again with one of the many nameless and faceless social workers. I do carry many more memories of foster placement number two as I lived with this family for fourteen months.

There was a mum, a dad, and one, two, three children all younger than me. A three bed semi-detached home on a more modern housing estate this time and the car sitting proudly on this drive had only three wheels. The Robin Reliant appealed to my sense of humour and the fact that it managed to have all the stability it required with only three wheels instead of the standard four was an interesting symbolism for me to ponder upon.

This was a very different kind of family, but similarly a grouping of people working hard to bring up their children, compelled for whatever reason to have an adopted child - the youngest one - and to foster angry, hurting teenagers. In bounces me.

The overwhelming sensation again is one of difference. I can't connect. I am disconnected. Disconnection is a huge part of this experience and indeed any experience that is painful. By this stage I am disconnected from myself. There is no anchor from which to centre my existence. I have no relationship with my mother, my gran is old and weary and for the life of her doesn't understand what is happening, and my uncle is raising his own family 300 or so miles away. I do not belong anywhere or to anyone; I just come to stay. I can stay a while in your life and you might care for me for a bit and feed me but I don't belong here now, do I? If I'm truly honest with myself, that sense has never left me, although I have created a deep sense of belonging for my own children, without whom I think I would be roaming the world, still looking for that beating heart that I belong to. They have taught me all I need to know about love and belonging, but I think I will always carry that particular set of stones in the metaphorical sack that I can pick up and put down whenever I wish.

I've arrived at this placement and they appear to eat pork chops, cabbage and mashed potatoes for their tea (a lot). I have never eaten food like this and it looks horrid and smells disgusting. In the kitchen they also have a hamster endlessly spinning around a wheel in a never-ending marathon of despair. I'd never had a pet in my childhood and I find it strange to see this little ball of brown fluff running around a wheel. So as my eyes dart round the kitchen, the hamster, the cabbage and the back door to the garden all capture my attention in a flick of an eye, the smell of soggy cabbage lingering on long after I've left the room.

The politics of food for children in care has become an even more fascinating subject for me since I have raised my own children. Food is such a personal thing. I don't think I had ever even seen a pork chop before I entered the second foster placement. Food politics is one of the very interesting things about being a child in care that would bypass most people unless they lived the experience. There is a connection between food and love, and also between food and identity. Food is a cultural thing and a class thing. This is pushed to one side in discussions when we think of children moving between houses and families.

One of the reasons that I cook up to three meals every evening is that I believe we should eat the foods we like, incorporating a nutritional balance of course! And I'm sure that this is a direct result of having no choice about food, what it was, how it was cooked, and with the knowledge that it was essentially something that people just 'do' so the differences, the politics of it, are not even considered. If you think about how your emotions and memories are connected to food, you'll probably find a whole heap of assumptions you've taken for granted, alongside some things that you had forgotten.

For example, if you think about your favourite meal, it probably has lots of associations to it. I remember roast chicken on a Sunday cooked by my gran, back during the first ten years of my life when I still lived with her. I remember the wish bone that nestled in the breast of the chicken, and of going off into the kitchen under the guise of getting a glass or using some other excuse and then picking chicken off the carcass whilst it was still warm. I try and cook roast chicken every Sunday now and I still pick the chicken off the bone whilst I'm dishing up and it still makes me feel delightfully naughty. I have no food associations I can recall in relation to my mother. It was my gran who cooked for me; her lovely onions, garlic and olive oil were directly connected to her being French, and she was way before her time in England when it came to food.

Each foster home and each children's home conjures up very different images of different food and I can tell you vividly about each one. Food is not to be ignored and yet I never remember anyone discussing food with me.

*

The time has come when the lovely foster parents can't cope with me anymore and my school can't cope with me either because I don't fit in there. I can't bloody cope with me but I'm rather stuck with me! That sensation of isolation, of otherness and of loss of self ran so deep within me that I remember feeling like I couldn't breathe. No amount of external pain would have made any difference to the way I felt. I could have been beaten black and blue and all I would have felt was that I was at least alive. It would not have hurt. I was beyond that. Living with the feeling of not belonging anywhere to anyone was quite enough pain to bear.

THE BRIGHTNESS OF STARS

The process of not 'fitting in' is twofold: I ensure that I don't fit in through creating an environment in which I can disconnect, and I really actually completely don't fit in. If I was ever 'different' before, I have now ensured my place of difference in stone. I am a child in care and I don't know anyone else in my school in the same situation. Well, who the bloody hell am I then? Where is my family? Is my dad looking for me so that he can take me to the place where I 'fit in'? No, because no one is looking for me. Not anybody.

Looking at life in hindsight can be revealing and forgiving but it can also be oh, so cruel. It is plain to see that no family environment would have been suitable for me. I had never had a father, a relationship that instils the notion of being looked after and having someone there for you who will protect you, a relationship that I have only fathomed in recent years. I didn't even know why there were men; three generations of single women parents and I can be forgiven for this lack of comprehension. I had lived as one of three hurting females, all scrabbling around looking for a protecting force in very different ways. Three generations of single parents with no understanding of their own pain. Alongside that, I had never had siblings, so the concept of sharing time and space with others was always going to be a challenging one, so again, I had to come to terms with the view that I was different, unable to fit in, that being me was not good, that I was always going to be rejected.

*

I'm in secondary school, perhaps coming towards the end of second year, maybe in third year. It has become quite apparent that my time at the girls' school is not really going to work out. Most lessons are spent in isolation. I have no desire to be a part of this hateful community and I want to die.

Moving from home to home and then school to school taught me many things but one of the outcomes of all of that movement was the knowledge that if you don't like something, you can change it. It's an interesting lesson as, on the face of it, this is a good thing. It prevents endless moaning about that uncomfortable shift of change, the inevitability of change, the acceptance of change as a part of life. It gives the individual the power to go and do something about things that need changing. From this starting point, everything can be dealt with, changed, removed. What I didn't learn in this place of power, control and wilfulness was that sometimes we have to work through things we don't like. We have to sit in the pain, the discomfort and the growth of not changing, moving or replacing. Sometimes it is by not changing something that the greatest of all changes comes about.

In families people often dislike each other, want time away or struggle with their differences and mostly, although not exclusively, they learn to forgive and tolerate and work with one another. In 'care', it really doesn't work like that (although again not exclusively, as some children settle into their families so much that they do indeed become one of the family for life).

To explore this further, I want to point out that all parties - and I mean absolutely everyone involved in the life of the child in care - can leave, move on, change the space – and ultimately everyone, except the child, is paid to be there. A social worker can get another job; a foster carer can say that things aren't working out; the school can request a managed move; the child/young person in question can ask to be moved (politely or through enforcing a breakdown of relationships). This is one of the unintended consequences of the system. There are many of these that will be highlighted in the course of this book and they are very much part of the impact of being in a system where everyone in your life is paid to be there. I believe some of the fallout from being a part of this system of change is an inevitability, and a completely different approach to looking after children who need looking after would be needed to avoid this, one that has yet to be thought of but would perhaps involve a model that had a mix of fostering and that of a children's home with potentially other on site opportunities in it rather than the 'either' 'or' approach that we currently have.

*

The new school is a mixed school maybe a mile away from the girls' school so everyone appears to know me and my reputation, whatever that was, travels with me in my school satchel. There's nothing 'fresh start' about this new building and I quickly fall into non-attendance, shouting matches with teachers, exclusions and 'non-engagement'. The breakdown of my second foster family placement coincided neatly with the second school asking me to leave. I think I was excluded although I can't be certain because the school might have wanted to avoid having the exclusion of a child in care on their records so it's highly possible that it was called a managed move again.

*

The professionals were running out of ideas and placements. With the breakdown of foster placement number two came the real cherry on the cake of the care experience in Northamptonshire in the 1980s – Tiffield. To some it was a home, for others a holding space. For me this was a terrifying set of three units filled with far angrier and far scarier teenagers than I ever was or had the potential to be. I was housed there for only two weeks but it may as well have been two years. I remember more about those two weeks than I do about places in which I lived for a year.

To try and engage myself in remembering some of the reasons why I was left with the feelings that I had about my two week stay in Tiffield, I decided to conduct some research. I wanted to see if it was still there or whether the building had been sold by the council to become a shopping centre or some other cathedral of despair built on top of the despairing memories held in the very soil upon which it stands - or something else, equally macabre. I also wanted to try and make sense of why it had left such a poignant bitter taste in my mouth.

During this process, I learnt things that I didn't know back in 1985 as a 15 year old girl. I found out that in 1996 it became a Secure Unit, a fact that answers many questions for me about the young people that I met in there. For while it was not necessarily a designated named Secure Unit, it was in the middle of nowhere and could only be reached by car, it had a noticeably high staff to young person ratio and its atmosphere was one of permanent volatility. Even during activities that appeared fairly 'normal', anger could burst out of almost any situation in the most unexpected of ways.

The definition I found for a Secure Unit is "a residential placement where you are locked up or prevented from leaving". That is very much how I remember it. It's a little like the sea that looked like a lake. Just because it looks like a lake doesn't mean it is so; if we all know that really it is the sea, why pretend that it is a lake? A child placed in a Secure Unit is usually, although not exclusively, awaiting a custodial sentence, is at risk of suicide, or is at risk of harming another.

Prior to being a Secure Unit, Tiffield was also a placement for anyone for whom there was nowhere else to go, alongside the self-harmers, the lost children, those awaiting sentencing and the suicide risks; all were likely residents. So you can call it what you like; it was filled with young people with those kinds of needs along with those of us who were simply waiting to find the next placement. I'm sure that there were others like me, others who had arrived in the place accidentally.

In Tiffield, we didn't go to school; schooling was on-site. Education took on a whole new meaning as this was really a classroom of containment. It was one room with desks and books and all of us were in there together regardless of age. I'm not even certain we went in there every day. We also did sports activities and had the odd singsong with a guy with a guitar.

One of the most interesting things that I have learnt about the human condition during all my experiences is that there is always a pecking order, there is always a hierarchy and there is always someone in charge of determining how that should work best. Divided we fall is more often than not the most likely way of operating. Together we stand only comes into play when there is an opposing force that sits outside your particular sub-group. It matters not where you sit in the societal spectrum as a whole; even if you are all lying on the ground in a heap, there is someone else lying at a slightly elevated level. There is always a hierarchy.

"We are all in the gutter, but some of us are looking at the stars."
Oscar Wilde

The way that this plays itself out among clusters of hurting, angry and abandoned young people can be very dangerous when unmanaged by the adults, who themselves may not always have the skills and life experience and support in order to deal with this well. The hierarchy expresses itself as a complex interweaving of sexual deviance, addiction capabilities, violence and offending.

Another discovery I made while researching Tiffield for this book was that there was a history of abuse at the home – not surprising really, given the climate and lack of 'care' given to those 'parented' by the Local Authority. During the mid to late 1980s two members of staff were arrested and later charged with sexual offences against girls in Tiffield, including rape and several counts of indecent assault. One of the workers in the home was described in court as a sexual predator, committing sexual offences on girls between 1985 and 1990. His offences were such that he was sentenced to 15 years in prison. [8]

The sex offender, who used the system that was designed to protect children as a place to assault and scar and maim the vulnerable, forgotten children in his care, was working in Tiffield the year I was there. He would take girls out on 'errands' and then rape them in his car in secluded areas. Sometimes he would go into their bedrooms and rape them there.

All of the information I have collected about my time in Tiffield has underpinned the feelings that I had while I was there and why I felt so frightened and vulnerable during my stay. This was an unsafe place to be on so many levels but I was dropped off here one day and left, once again wondering if someone was going to come and get me soon.

Young people who are in 'care' are vulnerable on so many levels. These children are forgotten children in forgotten buildings. This is why the adult voice of these people has to be heard and given exactly the same amount of value politically as the child's voice which, even with all the legislation and good practice guidelines in place, is also all too often a silent one. Is it any wonder that adults with such complex childhood experiences are more likely to find themselves within the mental health system or prison, or becoming victims of homelessness, poor educational attainments, depression or drug and alcohol addiction? And then there's the impact that this continued vulnerability has on the forming of

---

[8]

http://www.thefreelibrary.com/Sexual+predator+jailed+for+catalogue+o
f+care+home+abuse.-a0113959899

relationships in adulthood and repeated patterns of behaviour on their own children if their issues remain unresolved.

However, we have to remember that for some children, going into care is a saviour compared to the alternative offered by the family home, but the system itself leaves many of its children fighting their way through life at a cost to society that is too high to contemplate. Tiffield Secure Unit was closed down in 2007. May it rest in peace.

THE BRIGHTNESS OF STARS

THE BRIGHTNESS OF STARS

The Soundtrack

Material Girl - Madonna

Every Time You Go Away – Paul Young

I Got You Babe - UB40

You Spin Me Round – Dead Or Alive

Don't You (Forget About Me) – Simple Minds

The Headlines

Live Aid concerts

Brixton riots, sparked by the shooting of Dorothy Groce

Channel Four launched

The TV

Spitting Image

Eastenders

Happy Days

The Young Ones

*

THE BRIGHTNESS OF STARS

Remembered Moments

The Managed Move

It's 2003 and I'm sitting in a meeting with my 'social inclusion' hat on. It's quite an important meeting filled with head teachers, social workers, social inclusion managers and the like. I am there in the capacity of supporting one of the young people that I am working with who is at risk of being excluded from his secondary school. The discussion is about whether any of the other schools could perhaps take him. This is known as a managed move.

*

It's 1984 and I'm 14 years old and life at school, in the all-girls' school, is going horribly wrong. There is another school not far away, a mixed school. One of the many meetings held about me with my foster carers, social worker and teacher is about how it might help me to move to this other school.

Being in secondary school was one of the most unhappy times of my life and that system caused me as much damage as all the other systems that I was engaged in – to me they were all systems of exclusion, of ignorance, of rejection. When I think about school, I think about the word exclusion. Not only because that's invariably what happened to me in the end, but because that's the way I felt.

*

So I'm in the meeting with my work colleagues discussing this boy who we need to keep in the system and it dawns on me that this discussion had occurred about me: the managed move discussion. I sit there nodding, pondering to myself what it might be like to tell everyone around the table about my managed move, and I chuckle to myself about the irony of it all.

*

THE BRIGHTNESS OF STARS

Chapter Five
1986

They have found me somewhere else to go. My two week externally imposed prison sentence at Tiffield, which I am going to assume was given to me because of a lack of suitable provision elsewhere, was now finally coming to an end.

I can breathe. I no longer need to hold my breath for fear that I will be hurt, or for fear that no one will come and get me. My only hope, a social worker with an expanding caseload and a Ford Fiesta, has come to take me away. Here I come, Chalcombe Avenue. After so many moves I actually have no recollection of how long I was here, though a complicated calculation reveals it was probably about nine months.

The home was in a residential area, nestled among all the other houses, integrated into the lives that the TV was showing. Originally two semi-detached houses, they had been knocked together to create a seven or eight bedroom house to house us 'lost children' and I spent some time fascinated by the idea that you could enter the building from either front door of what would have been two separate addresses. My memories of this place are of drinking, diversity, complexity and misunderstanding.

The food there was cheap. Back to the food politics: there was no one making any nice home cooked food here. I remember eating little else but skinny white bread, toasted, soaked in butter, jam and peanut butter. The larder looked like a traders' warehouse like Costco, or a Kwik Save shelf (the Aldi of the 1980s). Endless jars of Happy Shopper jam lined the shelves and because all the food was bought in bulk the packaging looked different to anything you'd find in a supermarket. I can picture that row of food so vividly.

THE BRIGHTNESS OF STARS

This was a 'children's home' in the truest sense. The office was a pokey space the workers would hide and confide in, and in my imagination I visualised them all smoking our confiscated cigarettes. When the staff came to work they were in care too; they just didn't realise it. The walls were Institution Cream (aka Magnolia) and lacked anything that made it a family home. There were no pictures of people having a good time, family groupings, achievements; just empty walls, with the occasional room decorated with incredibly ugly swirly wallpaper.

In this home what stood out was that all of us were completely different. None of us fitted in anywhere and that, in a strange way, allowed us the opportunity to 'fit in' here. The group of young people in here were a mix and a half. I remember some having learning difficulties, one had behavioural problems; culturally and racially we spanned at least three continents and mentally we were all differently disturbed.

My education had been reduced to a tutor and playing computer games at a special unit, somewhere that I cannot recall the name of. By now I was officially being contained. Social Services just needed me to get to sixteen to move me on and to eighteen without me killing myself and causing a scandal. I was now associating with some very dangerous people, including a young man who has since spent most of his life in prison, most recently, I believe, for armed robbery to fuel his drug addiction. (I last heard of his whereabouts - a prison - in about 2002.)

There were also people like me, accidentally in a system we should never have been a part of, but somehow we didn't stick together – we were too caught up in a permanent fight with ourselves, society and everyone around us. We were no support network for one another and such a thing was never encouraged. Besides, I was destined to live in the tower block that we could see from the window of this 'jam jar home for the alone', with a baby – my keyworker told me so while pointing at it.

*

Although I was unable to articulate it at the time, the two mental states that I learnt to live with during the care experience were **fear** and **survival**.

fear

noun

1. a distressing emotion aroused by impending danger, evil, pain, etc., whether the threat is real or imagined; the feeling or condition of being afraid. **Synonyms:** foreboding, apprehension, consternation, dismay, dread, terror, fright, panic, horror, trepidation, qualm. **Antonyms:** courage, security, calm, intrepidity.

2. a specific instance of or propensity for such a feeling: *an abnormal fear of heights*. **Synonyms:** phobia, aversion, bête noire, bogy, bogey, bugbear. **Antonyms:** liking, fondness, penchant, predilection.

3. concern or anxiety; solicitude: *a fear for someone's safety*.

4. reverential awe, especially toward God: *the fear of God*. **Synonyms:** awe, respect, reverence, veneration.

5. something that causes feelings of dread or apprehension; something a person is afraid of: *Cancer is a common fear*.

sur·viv·al

noun

1. the act or fact of surviving, especially under adverse or unusual circumstances.

2. a person or thing who survives or endures, especially an ancient custom, observance, belief or the like.

3. *Anthropology* (no longer in technical use) the persistence of a cultural trait, practice, or the like long after it has lost its original meaning or usefulness.

This was an environment where my risk-taking behaviour could really grab me by the arm and show me places I never want to see again. My drinking was now daily, my self-loathing a natural state, eating rarely took place – this was to be the first of many places that I thought was my rock bottom until I learned that my emotional pain threshold was so high that I could go far lower than this and I did, again and again and again.

*

As I said, when a child has been in the care of the local authority, there is much more of a statistical presence in mental illness, in the prison system, in homelessness, in addiction and in unemployment. The extensive research that has proved this to be so created an environment whereby the Children Act 1989 could be born, with its very own interested and committed Section (24) that sought to attempt to redress the balance. For some, this was too late and from a personal perspective, it was far too late for me.

One of the features of families, however strange and dysfunctional they may be, is an element of responsibility. It's a spectrum, of course, but nevertheless there is someone there to pick up the pieces of any mess or disasters made during the formative years. One of the most horrendous aspects of this care system was that when I messed things up, as even the most balanced of teenagers are prone to do (and I was far from balanced), it was down to me. There was no one there. With no support network and a completely broken down relationship with my mother, who was now settled in a new relationship, a grandmother who was in her seventies and an uncle who was focused on raising his own family, I was filled with a complete feeling of aloneness in the truest sense. Since that time, I have always considered myself alone, without family and with nowhere to go should I need to.

There was no one to pick up my endless pieces, scattered as they were across the land, highlighting a brightly coloured trail of destruction and devastation.

During the summer of 1986 I was officially allowed to leave school but by this time I hadn't set foot in a mainstream classroom for nearly two years. My educational experiences were peppered with short spells of home tutoring, on site 'schooling', work placements and Referral Units. I can almost picture myself staring at a school leaver's certificate at the grand old age of sixteen with an emerging alcohol problem, living in accommodation that was desperate to teach me the skills required for moving on to 'Independent Living' so I could free up a much needed bed space, and with no support network whatsoever. How did I get here? How does a little girl with a ponytail and a teddy end up in a place of such self-destruction?

So my time in care was coming to an end and preparations for leaving the final children's home have begun. Prior to the Children Act 1989, I recall these 'preparations' being something of a token gesture. I remember being given my £27 per week allowance and shown how to cook a jacket potato and an omelette. (These were, in fact, incredibly helpful skills as living on £27 per week to buy food and pay bills, etc. meant that basically I was a very slender young person.) In fact the best way of managing the unmanageable was to forgo eating altogether and concern myself with other, more important diet staples such as cigarettes and alcohol. If I had these, then hunger didn't matter. If I had these, then paying the bills didn't matter. If I had these, then my life didn't matter. By the time I was sixteen I had learned the art of self-medication and I could ensure that in fact, most things didn't need to matter.

Social Services did try and house me, in an independent unit that was supposed to have a member of staff but I don't remember one being there, ever. There were several of us bright young care leavers though, all nursing our emotional baggage and our inability to communicate. I don't remember being there very long. But I do remember spending most of my pitiful allowance on food and feeling very pleased with myself at my very good budgeting skills, only to have it all stolen by the other residents. I couldn't prove it but one day I thought I would ask whether my food was being taken and my room door was forced open, I was punched about the face until the blood covered everything and that was that. I walked around the streets with my face covered in blood. No one came. No safety for me. I don't know what happened next. A short stay in a YWCA, a move to the Midlands to lodge at a social worker's mum's house. It's all a bit of a blur but then I ended up in a shared house in Wolverhampton.

In 1986, I came out of care no-one's responsibility, with no support, no money, and no home. Homelessness really was part of the whole package.

*

THE BRIGHTNESS OF STARS

THE BRIGHTNESS OF STARS

The Soundtrack

Rock Lobster – B52s

West End Girls – Pet Shop Boys

Chain Reaction – Diana Ross

Rock Me Amadeus - Falco

Papa Don't Preach - Madonna

The Headlines

John McCarthy is kidnapped in Beirut

Another Royal Wedding

Chernobyl disaster takes place

First test tube twins are born

Freddie Starr doesn't eat a hamster!

The TV

Miami Vice

The Cosby Show

Dynasty

The Flintstones

Prisoner Cell Block H

THE BRIGHTNESS OF STARS

Remembered Moments

Who Can Save Me?

I was involved in a 'managed move' from one school to another (excluded), an exclusion from the second school, and my shoplifting habit had taken hold so I became quite good friends with the Juvenile Liaison Officer, now part of the Youth Offending Team.

There are very few places to go when you hit this particular road of destruction at such a young age; in fact it's a slippery road, it spirals and it goes downhill very fast. It is clear now that each experience placed me one step closer to the next frightening and socially unacceptable place. Everyone could see it, I could feel it, but no one could stop it – my most frightening years.

*

THE BRIGHTNESS OF STARS

THE BRIGHTNESS OF STARS

Chapter Six
1987 - 1989

I really thought I'd seen the worst, that I'd felt the worst I could feel and stooped as low as I could go - and then came the experience of being homeless. An inevitability of being in care in the 1980s was the enforced period of total exclusion from society. I'm sure there were the lucky ones during this time but this was a world before the Children Act 1989 and The Children (Leaving Care) Act 2004. This was a time where children left care at 16. I was taken shopping with my social worker and we bought cups, cutlery, towels, bed linen and an iron. It was such a fun trip spending all that money but in real terms, that was it. A few shopping bags of household items, a conversation about buying food and a bed in a shared house that was doomed to fail.

This was not a time of supporting young people through education or hanging on to them until they were 18. This was not a time when knowing where the location of the young people in your care was a priority and was measured, with information demanded by the authorities. Times have changed, this is true, but having been in care - even with all the knowledge we have now - is still one of the high risk factors that leads to homelessness.

*

If I were to associate a word with this experience, it would be detachment - for what else can a person do? It seems to me that removing yourself from yourself, creating an aloofness between you, yourself, the people around you and the particular experience that you are in, would be a very normal way of dealing with something incomprehensible.

THE BRIGHTNESS OF STARS

de·tach·ment

noun

1. The act or process of disconnecting or detaching; separation.

2. The state of being separate or detached.

3. Indifference to or remoteness from the concerns of others; aloofness: preserved a chilly detachment in his relations with the family.

4. Absence of prejudice or bias; disinterest: strove to maintain her professional detachment in the case.

For me to connect with what I was going through would have somehow endorsed it, accepted it, made it ok - and it was far from ok. As I said in the last chapter, I somehow ended up in Wolverhampton. I remember so little about the why and the how of it all but I know that I was brought to a house, but I have no idea who brought me here or how I ended up in this part of the country. I presume I must have had a social worker somewhere but I have no recollection how I came by a social worker in this town. In my memory, I don't remember having one outside Northamptonshire, but there we are. Maybe the authorities were alerted that I was still 'in care' when I was looking for accommodation and signing on for benefits so I could feed myself.

The area was called Witmore Reans and the house looked rather large. I only remember two people from the house. One was a woman that I didn't like at all. She had a child, a seven-year-old boy, and I felt very uncomfortable around her. And the other was a boy, a seventeen-year-old called Pete, and he became my boyfriend for about seven months.

*

THE BRIGHTNESS OF STARS

After Wolverhampton came Penzance. Again, I have no idea why this even happened but me and the 'boyfriend of about seven months' got on a train and went to the depths of Cornwall. In the three or four months that I was there, I lived in a Bed and Breakfast, a shared house, a changing cubicle in a disused swimming pool, a train carriage, a tent and a caravan. My most poignant memories of that time were of being homeless in the storms of October 1987 and ending up in hospital with pneumonia; reading Keep The Aspidistra Flying by George Orwell; using a launderette to stay warm; and being looked at as if I were vermin by the locals.

While the storm was blowing everything into disarray and uprooting cars and trees and flowers and people and dropping them in other places, I had my own internal uprooting going on. Belonging nowhere was now my home. I felt it. I breathed it. I carried it with me everywhere I went. There are two sides to this interesting coin. I can go anywhere and be whoever I want; I am free. Free from obligation, from expectation, from who you think I am. Of course the other side of this coin is one of deep aloneness and vulnerability but I inadvertently chose to take advantage of the former in all its glory.

A huge turning point came for me during the time of Aspidistra when I met a journalist from Shelter[9] who was doing a report on homelessness across the country. Even in the mess that was my life, she inspired me. I saw her – I really saw her; I observed her closely: how she spoke, what she wore. I thought about her house and what it might look like and what friends she might have. She was a journalist and she lived in London and I wanted her life.

---

[9] http://www.shelter.org.uk/

THE BRIGHTNESS OF STARS

After my spell in hospital, I got straight on a coach to Victoria in search of this life that I believed I should have. Gazing up at the sky, stunned by the amount of air traffic that London seemed to have, I was blissfully unaware that I had nowhere to go. But London loved me and I loved it back. In the same way that expats must attract other people from their motherland, I attracted other homeless people very quickly who may well have themselves taken the arduous journey and complex route by which one might expect to arrive in London as a homeless teenager. Soon I was also to meet the people who went on to help me. Initially some people I met at the station took me to a squat in Kings Cross - I think; I really can't remember. Very soon after that, I was introduced to a charity called Alone In London[10]. I quickly became part of the system that protected me and eventually got me off the streets.

I have incredibly vivid memories of my stay at Centrepoint Night Shelter[11] which, back then, was based on Shaftesbury Avenue. Considering it was a holding space and I was there for less than two weeks, I can picture the staff, the dorms, the people, the feelings and I can even smell the food. My memories of that fortnight centre around protecting myself from two extremes: the Jesus Army, and a pimp in a metallic blue Jaguar. Both used young people to 'groom' other young people, with the Jesus Army being slightly more tempting as they lured you into their van with food and hot tea.

The night shelter regime was such that between 8am and 8pm we had to stay outdoors, which left us huddling together in the Trocadero in Picadilly Circus, begging money from tourists and trying to avoid the seedier side of life. We had Luncheon Vouchers with which to buy food and drink for the day but inevitably they

---

[10] http://www.aloneinlondon.org/
[11] http://www.centrepoint.org.uk

were mainly used to purchase cigarettes. From 8pm we would arrive back at the night shelter where we were greeted with smiles and served amazing food. It was lovely, and such a relief after the coldness of the December air. This faceless love was always welcome.

The rooms were in dorms and the residents were mainly all male. There was the odd woman who stayed in my very own dorm as the 'guests' changed every night, but I was often the only girl. I don't remember ever having any problems with the boys at all but I remember thinking that some of them were far more vulnerable than I was and I looked on as the odd boy got lost in the blue Jaguar with the pimp and I didn't see them again.

From here, the system delivered a clear structure and I was happy for it to do so. Next came the short stay hostel, then the long stay shared house until finally I was found my gorgeous cockroach-infested 8th floor towerblock flat on Battersea Park Road where I remained for five years; I lived happily alongside the cockroaches, who were housed in a heating system that gave them the perfect ground for breeding. We didn't meet often but we knew that we were both there, tolerating each other's existences.

In the midst of all this, however, I found the homeless charity Shelter and I plonked myself in their Campaigns Department on the 5th floor. I loved my time at Shelter but I'm certain I must have been a terrible pain in the arse! My social skills were poor, I was angry, unstable and desperately lonely. But in the eight months that I was there as a volunteer, they unconditionally loved me without knowing it or probably even meaning to. I worked on Shelter's 21st anniversary birthday bash, during which I was photographed standing on a podium in Covent Garden with Jeremy Irons, gazing up at him in adoration – they used the picture on the front cover of their newspaper. They also paid me £40 to write an article in their magazine, Roof. So here I am: I'm 17 years old and I am a journalist living in London! Hooray! There was still oh, so much more distance to travel - but this was a little nudge towards me feeling that maybe I was worth something after all.

*

Being housed in the cockroach-infested flat in Battersea in 1988 finally brought to an end two years of homelessness. As well as the nights spent in the B&B, shared house, changing cubicle, train carriage, tent and caravan in Cornwall I'd also slept on people's floors, in a squat, in a bus station, in a launderette, at a hostel, in a bedsit, on a bench and, of course, at the Centrepoint night shelter.

I had been spat on and called names, I'd felt a coldness in my bones I wouldn't wish on anyone and I had a permanent ache in my belly for food. Every day I was at risk. I was a young woman with an emerging alcohol problem, living in fear of what might happen next. Being homeless is tantamount to being the very scum of society, an experience that still sends me cold when I think about it. These were dark years indeed.

*

There are lots of misconceptions about homelessness and what it actually means. To be vulnerably housed does not mean that someone is necessarily a rough sleeper. To have nowhere safe to go, to feel unsafe where you are, to know that the accomodation you're in is temporary or that you could be thrown out at any time: this is to be homeless. I found this explanation which seeks to untangle the complexity of homelessness:

"Our Survey of Needs and Provision showed that there are approximately 43,000 people living in hostels and other supported accommodation for homeless people. In addition to this, there are people who do not show up in any official figures. These

include individuals and families who become homeless but find temporary solutions by staying with friends or family. This group is often referred to as 'sofa surfing' or concealed households. Others live in squats. Crisis has made attempts to quantify the level of this 'hidden homelessness', however this figure does include people living in hostels.

Some groups are more vulnerable to homelessness because they have particular support needs or have fewer rights. You are more likely to become homeless if you have:

- o *been in care as a child or had a disturbed childhood*
- o *a mental illness or addiction*
- o *been in the armed forces*
- o *spent time in prison*
- o *migrated to this country from Eastern or Central Europe or arrived as an asylum seeker." 12*

Since the day that I arrived in my flat on Battersea Park Road, I have never lived in vulnerable housing ever again. I made a very big and real commitment to myself that I would never let that happen to me again and that no one would ever take my home away from me. The feeling of vulnerability when you're homeless – the feeling of having absolutely nowhere to go - cannot really be explained but I can tell you that living without safety for any period of time changes the very core of you and adds imprints to your soul that will never be removed.

*

---

12 This is taken directly from www.homeless.org.uk who represent and support 500 organisations working with homeless people in the UK.

THE BRIGHTNESS OF STARS

The Soundtrack

It's A Wonderful Life - Black

I Don't Want To Talk About It – Everything But The Girl

Ride On Time - Black Box

Been Around The World – Lisa Stansfield

I Got You Babe – UB40

The Headlines

Terry Waite is kidnapped

Gunman in Hungerford kills 14 people

Thatcher wins an election for the third time

'Black' Monday – the Stock Market crashes

Storms are unpredicted by Michael Fish

The TV

No idea....

THE BRIGHTNESS OF STARS

Remembered Moments

The Phone Box 1987

I'm standing in a phone box in Soho, London. There are adverts all over the tiny square glass windows advertising sexual services. I didn't know I was in Soho or what that actually meant and I'm not sure I'd ever seen an advert about sex before. I phone my Uncle and tell him where I am. I've arrived in London and I'm homeless in London, in a phone box but I'm ok, I tell him.

*

THE BRIGHTNESS OF STARS

Chapter Seven
1990

I have many recollections of drunken comas. In particular, I remember lying in the middle of the road after drinking almost a bottle of gin, surrounded by people trying to get me up. My recollection of that experience is especially vivid partly because I never touched a drop of gin again. I was 14 years old. Don't blame it on the alcoholic, blame it on the gin! Within that fourteen month period of foster home number two, I cemented my addiction to cigarettes, found marijuana and, while I drank slightly less during this period, I knew by now that alcohol was available to me to change the way that I felt – the alcoholic's dream!

*

Once I had left 'care' and was homeless, drinking became a natural way of life. It keeps you warm and it keeps you numb. To sit on the edge of life, of society, of acceptance is not something that one really wants to fully feel. Drink and marijuana dealt with that nicely for me. Self-medicating had been my trusted friend but it had now become an arch enemy and wanted far more from me than I was prepared to give.

*

I'm 20 years old. It's Saturday 21st December 1990 and I've gone into the pub at around 5pm for 'a' drink. At this time I've just started studying at college for two A Levels with help from the charity Buttle UK. I have been housed so I am living in stable accommodation for the first time in years. I'm quite lost in London really but I don't care because I'm starting to get somewhere. I'm trying so hard to get my life into some kind of order and so many of the jigsaw pieces are falling into place for this to happen. All but one: alcohol.

THE BRIGHTNESS OF STARS

I 'come round' at around 3am. I am on my bed in my flat and there are strangers here and I don't know how I got home or how they got in. I've had a blackout. I'm scared but I can't move. I wake up again at 6am and get up, ready to go to work to start my shift. There is only me here now and I know that I cannot go on or I will die.

A blackout drunk is one of the worst experiences that alcoholic drinkers have; people have killed during blackouts. It's a complete loss of time in your life. You have no idea what has happened or where you have been. AA meetings are full of people talking about the terror of blackout drinking.

Word in the rooms of AA is that divine intervention supersedes a connection when it comes to Alcoholics Anonymous. I can't argue with that. At 20, I had never heard of AA before, let alone knew how to find them, but sure enough on that Saturday when I returned from work, I picked up the Yellow Pages and phoned them.

A voice asked me for my name and whether I would like anyone to come to my house to talk to me. Absolutely not! But I did learn that there was a meeting at 10pm that very evening, just off the Kings Road in Chelsea. That was my first meeting and that was also my first day sober - and I haven't had a drink since.

AA took the very broken me and pieced me back together, re-wiring me with emotional intelligence, affirmations, self-awareness, self-love and forgiveness, all through a sober looking glass. It was incredibly painful, albeit slightly less so than continuing the way I was living. It's fair to say that I had no idea that I was even going through all of this for a very long time. But that day in December marked the end and the beginning all at once and I shall take to the grave the gratitude I feel for the gift of sobriety.

THE BRIGHTNESS OF STARS

For a number of years life became a daily routine of AA meetings (sometimes up to three a day) alongside university lectures, and endless meetings after the meetings, otherwise known as emotional outpourings and sobriety conversations in coffee shops across London. And while I chose to take the 'bridge to normal living' that AA offered - which means that I haven't been to a meeting for many years - AA gave me a key: a key to my life, for which I will remain grateful forever. Life had begun, finally.

THE BRIGHTNESS OF STARS

The Soundtrack

Hotel California – The Eagles

Pink Floyd – Wish You Were Here

Groove Is The Heart – Deee-lite

Dire Straits – Romeo and Juliet

Ride On Time – Black Box

The Headlines

Poll Tax causes demonstrations

The Berlin Wall is torn down

Nelson Mandela freed from prison

Hillsborough claims 96 lives

Tiananmen Massacre

The TV

Still no idea....

THE BRIGHTNESS OF STARS

Remembered Moments

The Blue Bottle

One of my earliest memories is of drinking a bottle of medicine; a lovely blue bottle of medicine. I've always thought it rather strange that I could recall the colour, but it sat on the edge of my mother's bed in Zetland Street. We shared a bedroom and it had two single beds in it, a little like a hotel room or a dormitory, and the beds had very 1970s orange eiderdowns on them. This was life before duvets and it was all sheets and eiderdowns and endless work and skill involved to make the bed. It was a Victorian house and each bed, backed up against the wall, seemed to have its own window to look out of.

There can't have been a security cap on this bottle as I drank the lot. To this day I have no idea what it was or what it was for but the memory is so vivid as, upon realisation of the bottle's emptiness, I was dragged out of bed while sleeping and thrown over the sink with my gran's fingers down my throat while my mother held me, encouraging me to vomit out the bottle's contents.

As I write this down I sigh a very big sigh. That experience for me was so violent and aggressive yet fuelled by the good intention of keeping me alive and getting the horrid medicine out of me. This poor understanding of me as a real human being, affected by the world around me, dogged the parenting style of both the women who looked after me for those first ten years. Clumsy, thoughtless and overpowering, leaving a large footprint on my memory bank.

*

THE BRIGHTNESS OF STARS

THE BRIGHTNESS OF STARS

PART TWO

For each person who contributed their story to this book, I felt drawn to a particular area that I recognised as a part of what we might have dealt with as someone who has been in care either as a child, a young person or an adult.

Every story seemed to have a key element that stood out, and I've defined those elements to associate a single word with each story. In some instances, the words I have associated with each person are positive whereas for others the word is more about the healing process. All the words make sense to me and my story; I wonder if that will be the same for other people who have had similar experiences. Clearly we are never going to experience anything in a one dimensional way but ...

The words I have used are:

Education
Recovery
Identity
Connection
Strength
Resilience
Integrity
Visibility

Every word makes sense to me and I'm sure the voices you will hear in the next few chapters will also feel an affinity to all of these words through what they have gained, lost and recovered during their experiences. However, you may see and feel different strengths and emotions as you read their stories, but please understand that the words I have chosen are words of recovery and strength, not of pain and weakness.

THE BRIGHTNESS OF STARS

Chapter Eight
Tim - Education

Tim was taken into care at a very early age. His mother was already in the grip of the mental health service and that gave clear entry for intervention. However, the lack of stability that he was to endure prior to a full care order being taken on him at the age of 12 can't have been easy. Despite this, essentially he describes his experience of being in care as one of great success. A loving and stable long term foster placement, the financial backing supplied under current legislation to support his formal education and his own determination to succeed have meant that Tim has thrived and become the man he wanted to be.

He is one of the younger contributors of the book and his story couldn't be more different than that of just about anyone else I spoke to. In a way, he is proof that stability, which he was afforded from the age of 12, and financial support given to gain an education can help certain young people in a powerful and life changing way. In my experience, Tim's is an unusual story - even though many Local Authorities would like to bill it as though it were much more common than it actually is. Tim's story is certainly one for Local Authorities to aspire to.

ed·u·ca·tion

noun

1. The act or process of educating or being educated.

2. The knowledge or skill obtained or developed by a learning process.

3. A programme of instruction of a specified kind or level: driver education; a college education.

4. The field of study that is concerned with the pedagogy of teaching and learning.

5. An instructive or enlightening experience: Her work in the inner city was a real education.

*

Tim's story

"I came into care at around 3 years of age, my wonderful 'life story book' informs me. Unfortunately, my mum had developed mental health issues at a rather young age, and as time went on her condition became worse, to the extent where she felt it extremely difficult to cope and look after her children. My dad barely lived up to his parental responsibilities and I only caught glimpses of him in my life.

My mum and dad split up early on, as she, I suppose, realised that he was simply useless, and an awful man. When they separated he never appeared to care, seek contact or contribute anything to the children he had with my mum; there were three of us altogether, and he had two kids with another woman. My mum would have times where she was well and was able to cope, but it was the pregnancies that seemed to trigger her mental health issues and there would be times where she would have to be sectioned under the Mental Health Act. With no suitable alternative arrangement, all of us children would then have to go into care.

I spent from the age of 3 up until the age of around 12 going into care, and then back home, into care, and then back home, which must have happened a good 15 times; again, my Life Story Book tells me so. Eventually it became quite apparent that my mother was never going to be able to cope. My mum did battle it out in court; however, she lost her battle, and Leicester City Council subsequently took parental responsibility. Long term care orders were placed upon her children, and it was not too long after that my brother Rob and I were placed in a long term foster placement, where we lived for around 9 years before heading off to university. We were separated from my other brother, who was given a foster placement elsewhere.

I can honestly say, and I feel forever grateful for this, that when I left care I felt ready to leave. I felt that I had been equipped with the skills to live independently; I had a full time job, and I was renting accommodation with my brother Rob. This day came, I think, back in April 2011, and that was finally it, I was living on my own two feet. Actually I feel like I parted from what many would call my 'corporate parents' when I headed off to university, as by this point I had fairly little contact with either my leaving care support and development worker or my foster carers anyway. The leaving care services that I received under S24 of the Children's Act were, I must say, extremely helpful, and I am totally grateful for this support. I did not have to worry about costs associated with the tuition fees, or accommodation, and what's more, I received various grants that assisted me further with the costs associated with going to university.

I always aim to remind people that without this support, things could have been so very different. I hope that the investment put into me was worth it and as a result of this investment, I would like to think that I will certainly pay all of those costs back. I will be paying my taxes until I retire, as will my children too, because the cycle has been broken.

Unfortunately there are still many care leavers who continue to need society's resources because they didn't have that investment, and sometimes it can be a very difficult cycle to break. Unfortunately there are young people placed into care who do not necessarily get the same deal as I received. I often say that it can sometimes be like a lottery – it's the luck of the draw what deal is handed to you. But I also believe that you're the one that can make that change.

I can only say that for me, being placed in the care of Leicester City Council has affected me in a positive way, as I feel through being care experienced I have adapted to transition far easier, become that bit more confident than most, and I have developed a mentality which encompasses a 'work hard now, it will pay off later' attitude.

Since becoming a care leaver, I have been employed by a vast amount of employers, though I've only changed jobs because of going backwards and forwards from university. I have had no trouble in terms of developing friendships and sustaining those friendships. I have now found my ideal career and I am heading back off to university to study Social Work. I've purchased my first property with my brother, which has gone really well. Never did I think that I would live in a brand new 3 bed detached house with a nice garden and garage – let alone own a house, although I must admit that my late grandmother significantly contributed to making this happen, as she was the one who gave us the deposit we needed.

If I had not been placed into care, I can only think that my life may have turned out a little differently. Perhaps I would not have achieved what I have done; you never know. I am just ecstatic about finding out what life will bring me now.

As I have already alluded to a little, having to mature faster than my non-looked-after peers has, without a doubt, propelled me to work hard. Not only that, having to deal with change and transition on so many occasions has made it a far easier process when embarking on my university journeys, moving house, and starting new jobs, quite simply because I'm used to it. Going through the care journey, you do come into contact with a vast amount of professionals, deal with change, get familiar with the need for procedures and protocols, so you actually learn a fair bit. Another consequence of me experiencing all of this, for me anyway, is that my social skills are strong, as is my confidence and my ability to communicate and voice my opinions to others.

I would highlight independence here. It was clearly very evident when going off to university that my housemates (brilliant guys, by the way) were not as clued up or as streetwise as I was. I can recall taking my housemate food shopping, and he really didn't have much of an idea, he didn't know where things were, or what to buy. Furthermore, when it came to sorting out domestic tasks in the house, and dealing with the bills and correspondence, this was something else that I dealt with, as this was what I was used to. This was certainly a strength that I had, which ironically I developed as a result of being 'looked after'.

My housemates came from extremely privileged backgrounds, and for me there was a real sense of achievement to think that I had reached the same level as them. Despite my adverse background, we were at the same university (University of Leeds), studying the same course (BA Sociology and Social Policy), and we all achieved the same result, a 2:1. (Actually, they both did straight Sociology, so it could be argued that my subject was a little harder because some modules touched on social policy!)

My housemates were aware of my background, and I do feel that I made them think that bit more about people out there in the world who are disadvantaged, and of course I certainly made them appreciate that bit more what they had been dealt in their lives."

*

THE BRIGHTNESS OF STARS

Chapter Nine

Jane - Recovery

I was introduced to Jane by a close friend. He knew bits of her story and thought she would be a good person for the book. Jane's story blew me away. Her own journey into care was harrowing enough without the late 1960's and 1970's approach to children in need of 'care'.

re·cov·er·y

noun. (pl. re·cov·er·ies)

1. The act, process, duration, or an instance of recovering.

2. A return to a normal condition.

3. Something gained or restored in recovering.

4. The act of obtaining usable substances from unusable sources.

Jane is 50 years old and has a story that is harrowing and unbelievable in equal measure yet this successful woman sits before me, kindly offering to share that which has been unspoken for a long time.

*

"As far as social services and the police were concerned, the reason that my sister and my brother and I were taken into care was because we didn't attend school for a year. We were homeless which meant that we moved about an awful lot. We also had no money, because we were homeless and my mother couldn't get any support because we were outside of the system, so to bring in money, she became a sex worker.

We moved about constantly and lived an unbelievably dangerous lifestyle because of some of the places that we ended up staying in. Some of the men's homes we stayed in my sister and I were abused by these men; so yes it was quite horrifically dangerous we were incredibly vulnerable and in desperate need of protection.

The background to us being homeless and not attending school for a year was quite horrific. I'd had a childhood full of abuse of all kinds. I was sexually abused by numerous abusers one of whom was my eldest brother. That had happened from, I would guess, about the age of 7 years old, but I don't really know.

My mother and father were never married, which was unusual in those days, but we were his second family. There were five of us children and he abandoned us when I was just 10 years old. We survived for a while because he was still supporting us financially as a family. Then my eldest brother, who was my abuser, got hit by a car and died when he was 17. I was then 12 and had just started high school.

Not long after my brother died, my mother sent us with a few belongings to a male friend of hers, with a note, for him to look after us and she attempted suicide that night. So she was hospitalised and we were farmed out by my father to different members of our extended family. My Dad was back on the scene again for a short time. While we were staying with these family members and Mum was in a psychiatric hospital receiving electric shock treatment, my Dad sold our family home, had a huge bonfire and destroyed all our belongings. She could do nothing even when she was well enough, because they weren't married.

So, she came out of hospital and we were homeless – we had nothing and nowhere to go. We stayed with the same male friend of hers for a while in an over-crowded council house. This was the year we were homeless, moving around, being abused. I remember phoning for ambulances as my mother was physically beaten, regularly by her boyfriend/pimp. He was also one of my sexual abusers. He went on years' later to murder a man in a row over the price of a can of soft drink. At last he was sent to prison.

I arrived into care and the one thing I remember was feeling safe. At last I was safe. My sister and I felt that really strongly, it was safe and she wasn't around. The dreadful thing about it was that we were separated from my brother who was 6 years younger than me, so he was 6 years old – just a child.

In those days, if you were in care long term, it was separate children's homes – in Walsall there was a home for boys and a home for girls. The impact of that decision is that I don't really know him. My sister and I are very close – she left for London when she was 16, she ran away. So she has less of a relationship with my brother than I do and I don't have a good relationship with him, I don't know him.

Even though we felt safe, I have abiding memories of a loveless environment. I vividly remember the regimentation, the type of institutional obsessions with certain elements of everyday life which helps the institution run more smoothly for staff, but is not child centred! For example, we had a very early wake up (around 6.30 which was when morning staff came on duty) followed by a strict rule about getting up, using the bathroom, making beds and being downstairs in 20 minutes. The older children had to make the beds of younger girls, we had one or two each depending on the makeup of the ages of those in the home at any one time.

The beds would be inspected and torn apart if not up to scratch. All very much about power and control, reinforcement by the matron! I remember the younger child whose bed I had to make, used to wet her bed and we tried to sneak this past the matron, but this was very difficult because there were areas where anything was stored that were out of bounds (the implication was we were all thieves so permission was need for everything).

Inevitably this child, Sharon, (of about 5 years old) would be found out and she had to, for her punishment, hand wash her sheets in a bucket in the utilities area, while the rest of us had breakfast. The humiliation and damage done by this cruelty we can only guess at. I learned recently, two years ago in fact, that she had been a 'battered' woman all her life and was eventually murdered by her partner two years ago.

The 'little uns' as we called them, were lovely, I felt so sad for them. We tried to cheer them up as best we could. The matron had her favourites and she was quite open and obvious about it. They received preferential treatment and the rest of us looked on powerless. I believe that my feelings about fighting all injustice and racism began then. I've been told, because I don't remember, that when they all had chickenpox I read stories to them. I believe I probably did because I was always reading to myself and others. I see the teacher in me even then!

Every Christmas and Easter we had presents from local women who worked in local shops and factories, strangers who we never met. At first I didn't understand why we were seen as 'charity cases' I had never viewed myself from that perspective. But I understood it for the younger ones who I realised some of them had no-one outside. I never forgot their kindness and although they were anonymous they wrote our names on each gift card as if they knew us. It's meant that as an adult I have fostered difficult teens and supported children through organisations like Plan International and worked as a volunteer for various charities like Stepping Stones and Samaritans. I'll never forget 'from all the girls at Littlewoods' and 'all the girls at Crabtrees' and the thought that someone cared who didn't even know us.

The court order was rescinded when we got to the age of 15, for my sister and 16 for me. I understand this to be because we had been taken into care due to non-attendance of school, so as soon as the legal school leaving age was reached we were sent back home. Of course, the abuse started again straight away, for both of us. And this time it was the same boyfriend who had abused me who was now abusing my sister.

Having been in care meant that when I went back home, I knew that things had to be different and after many rows I was beaten and thrown out of the house. My sister ran away a few days later and she never came back.

We were still so very vulnerable and I had been targeted while I was in care by a man who was 6 years older than me. Very quickly I was pregnant. I think that I was looking for affection. Care is a *loveless* place, there is *no* love whatsoever in there, we didn't see it and we didn't find it. All we saw was more abuse. It was a different kind of abuse but abuse all the same.

So I was pregnant and in a very abusive relationship which unfortunately I have to say lasted 19 years. So for a further 19 years I was abused. I had low self-esteem and everything that goes with that and it took me that long to be able to work on myself and get myself together, so that I was strong enough to leave. Which I knew would be dangerously *horrific* and it was. But I was determined to leave – I wasn't taking it any more. I remember thinking 'Is this my life, is this it, is this all there is?'

What might have helped me and put the brakes on my living out the next 19 years in fear would have been when I was at first at home with my young children. I was determined to achieve my ambition to be a teacher and when they were toddlers, I started going to the local FE College one evening a week to evening classes to gain my A-Levels. That took 2 years and then I started teaching a bit of ESOL in a home tutoring, voluntary scheme. As soon as they were both at school full time, aged 5 and 6 years old, I got a place at a local university and studied for a degree and a teaching qualification. *That* would have been the time, because that was my real time of growth. But life took over with working, raising my children and managing the abusive relationship.

Education was the key for me; I loved it and I absolutely thrived on it and that is one thing I took into adulthood. I *love* learning and to go into teaching was just a natural thing for me, to pass on that love of learning and to help and empower others. I just love it. If anyone could have helped me with my personal development that would have been the time I think.

When I think about what I have gained from all of those experiences I think one of things about me is that I am resilient, no matter how many times I get knocked down, I get back up again. I don't think it's possible to can get to where I am now without it and that's one of the things about me that I am most proud. That is not to say that there haven't been times when I have wanted to end it all, because there have. Depression has presented itself a couple of times. I often feel like an outsider in groups of people. My experience separates me, but also connects me with others who have had similar experiences. I think we recognise something in each other. We've got through it all and come out the other side. I'm definitely a survivor."

*

THE BRIGHTNESS OF STARS

Chapter Ten
Noel – Identity

There is so much research around identity and the difference that is made when our identities are handled well that it begs the question why it still has to be highlighted as an area in need of further understanding - but it does. The discussions remain about improvements that need to be made to policies and procedures around Adoption.

i·den·ti·ty

noun

1. The collective aspect of the set of characteristics by which a thing is definitively recognisable or known: "If the broadcast group is the financial guts of the company, the news division is its public identity" (Bill Powell).

2. The set of behavioural or personal characteristics by which an individual is recognisable as a member of a group.

3. The quality or condition of being the same as something else.

4. The distinct personality of an individual regarded as a persisting entity; individuality.

5. Information, such as an identification number, used to establish or prove a person's   individuality, as in providing access to a credit account.

6. Mathematics

a. An equation that is satisfied by any number that replaces the letter for which the equation is defined.

b. Identity element

Feeling excluded will only ever ensure negative outcomes for children and young people as they develop and move through the transition into adulthood. The sense of not belonging to a group, a family, a school, an area alongside the differences experienced while being 'looked after' can cause a number of responses. A child or young person may choose to self-exclude as a means of protection, retreat into 'another world', seek out others with the same issues and form meaningful but often damaging alliances, or learn to self-medicate on drugs and alcohol, for example, rather than live with the sensation of isolation or even feel suicidal.

While this is going on at a level that is more easily accessible, the issues around identity regarding culture, religion and unidentified parents, for example, create a much deeper feeling of an unknown identity. Put these two places of unresolved states together and throw in some developmental confusion and general teenage angst as well and we have a very lost and hurt child/young person.

Noel found me on one of the Facebook groups that I am in after I started talking about this book. He sent me a message saying that he might be able to help me as he had been adopted. We arranged to meet in a pub in Chipping Norton and I asked him how I might be able to spot him. He replied, "Don't worry. I'll be the only man in the bar with dreadlocks. You won't miss me." Now if you've ever been to Chipping Norton in The Cotswolds, you'll appreciate how amusing a thought that is; it is the land of Middle England, The Hunt, golf and horse riding and where the Daily Mail is the paper of choice in most establishments. Much of Oxfordshire, the place I currently find myself living, could be described in this way without looking too deeply. So as he had suggested, Noel was indeed incredibly easy to spot.

*

THE BRIGHTNESS OF STARS

Noel's story

"Trying to piece together what happened and where I have come from has been tricky; it's a long time ago. I saw the court reports to do with my adoption and reading in between the lines, my birth mother was in a bad place. She gave birth to me and stayed in hospital for however long she had to, which in those days I'm guessing was about 4 or 5 days. She developed a pattern of leaving me there and coming back a number of times over a period of about 2 or 3 months, each time saying that she was going to take me home. Each time, she kept leaving me. In the end she just upped and left and never came back. She left me there for the authorities to deal with. And that's how I came to be in care with foster parents until subsequently I was adopted.

Again, looking at court reports - because obviously I was too young to remember - there was a lot of to-ing and fro-ing going on, but from what I can gather, *happy* to-ing and fro-ing. The court reports themselves make no mention of me being an unhappy child; I am always referred to as a *happy* child and one that someone would be quite happy to have. I would conclude from that that during those three and a half years where I was 'passed from pillar to post' I was actually *happy*. I think I was shown quite a lot of lightness and love. I am a happy person. I wake up every morning always thinking positively, thinking that something good is going to happen today and I think that is the best way to live your life. I think if you start off negative you tend to bring the world down around you, so I've always been happy; it's not an act, I don't go home, close the curtains and cry! I try to find the good in everyone.

I met my mum when I was fifteen years old. It really didn't help me in any way and in fact just brought more confusion. When I had read the reports about my adoption there were lots of mentions of siblings, and siblings being adopted out as well, and

THE BRIGHTNESS OF STARS

I'm actually a twin! He was adopted out too and I met him at that first meeting with my birth mother but I completely disregarded him. He was there because he was welcomed back into the family and I wasn't, and I was a bit unprepared for that. Because I was fifteen and dealing with my own 'stuff' as a teenager, trying to make sense of everything, I hadn't really prepared myself or done enough research. I was in too much of a rush; it was a very impulsive thing I did. But subsequently I have been back since around the time I was aged 29/30 and that was a lot better as I was more prepared. I also sat down and talked to my brother and I have talked to my mother *better*, although I still haven't quite got the answers. I very much doubt I'll ever see them again, but I got quite a lot more resolved because I was a lot older.

It was around 1991 when I made that first visit to my birth mother. As an adoptee trying to find the people that gave birth to you the avenues that were available to me were absolute rubbish. I really cannot see the point of withholding somebody's birth certificate; I really can't see the logic in that at all. I think anyone that gives someone up for adoption must always realise that at some point that person might come knocking on your door; it's just human nature, so why the government and everyone else turn their back on the poor person who never *chose* to be adopted out in the first place is beyond me. I had nowhere to turn to get help and no one seemed to know who exactly could help me. I think now that access to documents has got better, you know, you can now get your original birth certificate and that's not an issue, but I still don't think there is enough support there. No one helped me at all during that time and no one was remotely interested in what I needed to do and I'm not sure how much that has changed.

I must add at this point that I was very very lucky. The parents that adopted me were very organised, a 'belt and braces' family. They kept the driving licences in a box in the sideboard and they kept all my adoptive papers. I consider this to be a very lucky thing for me because had they not I would never have seen them. However, as I had no one helping me manage my need to meet my birth parents, I don't think anyone was helping my adoptive family either.

My mum was a teacher and my father was a youth worker. They were white and I am black. The whole interracial adoption was a lot easier back then and as a teacher and a youth worker, I don't think you could have picked two better professions. I think the courts just stamped the papers. I think the court just said absolutely, you've already got a daughter yourselves, you're obviously good with children, and away you go. I'm not certain that anyone ever sat down with them and said, do you know what? You love this child, you put plaster on his knees, you feed him, you clothe him, you cuddle him when he's upset. You do realise that at some point he might turn his back on you and try and find his birth mother? I don't think anyone ever told them that. So when I did need to meet my birth mother it seriously affected my relationship with them.

We are over it now, but it caused a massive rift for years. Looking back, we always thought it was something else, but that's where it stems from – this desire for me to go and see my mum - and they didn't stop me, they applauded it; they said you should do and here's all your paperwork. But they didn't know how to deal with it, I didn't know how to deal with it either and more importantly there was no one there to help us or tell us how to put the pieces back together afterwards. And I can see that when you bring someone up for 15 years, treat them as your own, give them everything they could possibly want and they say sorry, I'm off to find the person who gave birth to me, it must be so cruel. Of course at 15 I didn't know it had an impact on them. I wonder if the support network is there now. It was only a year or so after that I moved out of home and things were never quite the same again, although we did recover to a large degree but that took about eight or nine years.

During that time I never talked about all the things that were happening because I could never put my finger on that being the trigger and the catalyst for it. I didn't understand it all myself.

I have no idea about my dad and I haven't really delved into it too much. For me it is an unresolved issue. Is it because I want to know who he is? Is it because I want to make myself complete? Or is it purely just because it bugs me? I don't know. I wonder how much of me does actually want to meet my father. I would guess that actually, in a funny way, very little of me really does want to meet him. In the same vein *all of me wants to meet him.*

The best way I can explain it is to differentiate between want and need. Do I want to meet him? Do I need to see him? Do I *want* to see him? No, not particularly, I've lived quite happily for 36 years and I'll live the rest of my life happily without seeing him. Do I *need* to see him? Probably yes, because there will always be that element of doubt and upset. So yes, want and need are probably the best way to describe this conundrum. My mother was very tight-lipped and wouldn't say anything about him and his name isn't on the birth certificate, so unless she actually divulges who he was, I shall have to go to the grave not knowing.

I think everyone will always want to know where they came from; who their mother and father were, under what circumstances they were born etc. and I think everyone would feel that they have that gap in their life if they didn't know. I've *still* got that gap in my life and yes, it is going to leave some questions unanswered, which is inevitable unfortunately.

The main thing that stems from the *psychology* of being adopted is around not necessarily being wanted and of being on your own, which has always led me to be an individual and therefore just to go and explore the world. A lot of people like the safety blanket; they would never just get on a plane and go and live in Italy for 3 months or just go and put all their life savings on red on a roulette wheel. So as an adult I suppose I do gamble with life sometimes, because there has never been anyone there to say look, this is the right thing to do or this is the wrong thing to do; there were never any boundaries set.

By being given up for adoption and because of that lack of boundaries, I find myself wandering off. I am known for being a bit of a traveller and a wanderer – "have passport, will travel!" I believe that for me, that all stems from my adoption, because I lived without those boundaries.

The good side of that is that I look back at my passport and it's got some incredible stamps from all around the world, nearly every continent, some incredible parties and amazing people, some fantastic times and incredible memories and opportunities, things that people will never get to do. The sad side to all that is that I never quite finish anything though. My C.V. is full of one job after another, because I could never just stay there, because there were never the boundaries. So that's the one major thing that has affected me from being adopted, and that's boundaries.

I don't feel unique but some of the scenarios I come up against feel unique to me. When I've taken long haul journeys and I'm asked questions about my family medical history, of course I don't have a clue. I have absolutely no idea about my medical history. When I went on holiday to Jamaica, where I know my mum came from, I spent half the holiday thinking perhaps my nan lives in that house!

The biggest outcome from having lived the life I have is that I put up barriers. I absolutely believe that I put up barriers because - and it's totally cliché - I was abandoned by the person who was supposed to love me more than anyone else, and it is because of these barriers that I think friends have suffered. Partners have definitely suffered and it's not their fault but I won't open up to them; I just will not open up because of that fear of rejection and I carry that around with me everywhere I go, which is a terrible shame, and I'm sure that it stems from adoption."

*

Chapter Eleven
Dianne – Connection

Dianne found me on Twitter. I love Twitter so much and have made some amazing acquaintances and friends using this medium.

For me, Dianne is all about connection: connection to self.

connection

noun

1. the act or state of connecting; union

2. something that connects, joins, or relates; link or bond

3. a relationship or association

4. logical sequence in thought or expression; coherence

5. the relation of a word or phrase to its context in this connection the word has no political significance

6. (often plural) an acquaintance, esp one who is influential or has prestige

7. a relative, esp if distant and related by marriage.

*

Dianne's story

"Ironically, feeling like a 'nobody' as a child has helped me develop a strong sense of 'me'. I knew that whoever I was or wasn't, I was 'Dianne'. Whilst I didn't value her or believe that anyone else did she was the only person on the planet on whom I could rely. Not in a big loud in-your-face way but in a cool calm quiet way. As a teenager I was a real loner, spending most of those years alone both at home and at school. I developed the ability to be both physically present but emotionally absent at the same time. Protecting the gentle soul within.

Whilst spending all my childhood trying to please the adults around me in order to fit in and receive their love, I developed a strong sense of right and wrong. I needed to discover what was going to give me a smile and good attention rather than being ignored or worse. The positive side of being 'good' all the time was it saved me from sliding into the darker side of life.

I had several opportunities as an attractive young woman to take seemingly easier options to gain a comfortable lifestyle and receive 'love'. However, I appeared to have developed a strong moral sense; I knew where the line was and I wasn't prepared to cross it.

Whilst this was a fear based mindset I am sure ultimately it saved my life and more importantly maintained my integrity. This has stayed with me all my life. It is a strange dichotomy that whilst I didn't value who I was I knew that I had to keep safe all that I was.

I am grateful for that and I believe it is a direct result of my experiences as an unloved child.

I cannot count the times that people have said to me: "I can't believe you were in care, you seem so ... normal / well balanced." There is a perception that children in care come from backgrounds that are of a type. And those children will always emerge damaged from their homes and the system. For me the experiences of those years were indeed profoundly negative.

However, they were also a fertile ground for encouraging me to seek out the valuable, lovable me. Yes, there has been, and is, a lot of introspection; however, I have learned to love myself as I am loved by the many others in my life. My life has unfurled, petal by petal, revealing that gentle precious soul that had retreated to avoid decimation by the so-called carers around her.

I have a complete lack of bitterness about my experiences; I have come to accept that the key players all had their own 'stuff' going on. However, losing my mother at two years of age meant I lost the person who truly cherished me, the way I cherish my children. That loss was accompanied with indifference or neglect.

This has also allowed me to have an unerring ability to see both sides of any and every situation. I don't judge; I accept that everyone operates with what they have.

The biggest lesson I learnt from all of this was that I have a choice. I can choose to hate the people who caused me so much pain, turned their back on me and ignored my needs. I could have chosen to medicate myself through those years with one substance or another. I could have taken up some of the very dodgy offers of 'help' I was given. I could have chosen to turn my back on my values and do whatever I had to do to run with the crowd, any crowd. Instead, for the most part, I chose to observe and learn from everything and everyone.

I confess I didn't consciously decide I wasn't going to be defined by my experiences as a child until after I was married. Up until that time I realise now that I was doing that innately. When my children were born, however, I realised that I was looking through a filter of fear at every aspect of life and my strategy was to disengage when the going got tough.

I spent my childhood with people who had 'disengaged' from me; I wasn't going to do that with my precious babies. So I made different choices, every step of the way, re-engaging me with all the emotions I had been suppressing to survive. It was painful - but worth it.

I was a timid, unadventurous child and young person, never ever stepping outside my immediate comfort zone in any situation. However, ultimately my experiences have allowed me to live my life back to front. The freedom and love I didn't have as a child, I have now.

I am interminably inquisitive! Constantly curious, peering into new subjects, learning new skills and expanding my knowledge. The fear that kept me safe and confined in a controlled emotional environment has been a springboard to explore and engage in new experiences. I truly believe that life gets better, not worse.

Those formative years on my own without guidance and support have meant that eventually, with age, I have developed the growing confidence in myself and in my ability to make good decisions.

Now in my fifties, I am free to be me! Warts and all! I am more outspoken than ever before and not necessarily the 'pussy cat' I was, which inevitably brings different problems.

However, that's okay because finally Dianne has found her voice, and she likes the sound of it!"

*

Chapter Twelve
Carrie – Strength

I met Carrie while I was speaking at the Buttle UK Conference 2012 where she was leading a panel of young people in education as they told their stories to the delegates and shared their experiences of being in education as a child in care, both good and bad.

Strength

noun

1. The state, property, or quality of being strong.

2. The power to resist attack; impregnability.

. The power to resist strain or stress; durability.

4. The ability to maintain a moral or intellectual position firmly.

5. Capacity or potential for effective action: *a show of strength.*

6. a. The number of people constituting a normal or ideal organisation: *The police force has been at half strength since the budget cuts.*

b. Military capability in terms of personnel and materiel: *an army of fearsome strength.*

7. a. A source of power or force.

b. One that is regarded as the embodiment of protective or supportive power; a support or mainstay.

c. An attribute or quality of particular worth or utility; an asset.

8. Degree of intensity, force, effectiveness, or potency in terms of a particular property, as:

a. Degree of concentration, distillation, or saturation; potency.

b. Operative effectiveness or potency.

c. Intensity, as of sound or light.

d. Intensity or vehemence, as of emotion or language.

9. Effective or binding force; efficacy: *the strength of an argument.*

10. Firmness of or a continuous rising tendency in prices, as on the stock market.

11. Games Power derived from the value of playing cards held.

I particularly like 'source of power' definition of strength in relation to Carrie although I'm not certain she recognises this for herself yet - but passing through the years will assist her in this revelation.

*

Carrie's story

"I was first involved with Social Services at around the age of 9/10 when I was recognised as a 'neglected child'. Me and my two brothers - one is a year and a half older and the other is 9 years younger than me - were put on the 'At Risk' register.

It wasn't until I was 11 that I became fostered. I went into foster care a very damaged young girl who felt wholly responsible for my mother's welfare and spent a long time feeling resentful that I had been taken away from her. It is hard to even remember my state of mind at this time, but in reflection and reading reports written at the time by social workers I recognise and remember key points.

I remember being sat down and spoken to about moving out of my mother's and at the time it was a 'temporary' situation. However, the extent of my damage was assessed and that, combined with a deterioration in my mother's behaviour after I left, determined that a permanent move would be the most beneficial for my development mentally and physically. I've tried to blank out the memory of one of her actions that proved that her children shouldn't be living with her: she slit her wrists when my brothers and I moved out. After she did this she came to where we were and told us that it was our fault because we didn't live with her. She was put in a mental health institution after this event for a period of time.

I have moved on massively from the young damaged girl that I was, but I know certain things still affect me now, but this just means that I have more growing and healing to do, which is to be expected of someone who is only 24.

It wasn't until I was 17 that I decided enough was enough, and I decided I wanted more from life, and to be treated better. At the time this was with regards to my education; my school knew I was a Looked After Child as I was on a 'special' list, yet from the supposed support I received from the school, you wouldn't have known. The point I decided I had had enough was when they told me that they didn't expect me to pass any of my A Levels, and that they weren't bothered if I went to the classes and did no work, but I had to attend the lessons or they wouldn't get paid for me. I still now think, "WOW, how the hell did they think saying this to me would be beneficial to either party?!" This was the turning point in my life, which let me move forward and start to heal myself. This meeting happened because I had not been going to my lessons or doing as much work as I should as I was deeply depressed and was dealing with my mother attempting suicide on Boxing Day because 'she had nothing to live for'. I made them aware of what had happened and no support was offered, just a ultimatum given.

I wouldn't ever change my past even if I could. I am the person I am today because of my past, and I have managed to create a positive life from a negative environment.

THE BRIGHTNESS OF STARS

When I first went into care, I trusted no one and watched every movement of every person around me, trying to read their next move. I struggled with friendships and always felt like an outsider looking in; this of course may have been partly down to my chronic depression that went undiagnosed for years. I could say something to someone, and then spend a week worrying about the effect of what I had said, when really the person I said it to didn't even remember it an hour later. This is the negative side; I constantly have to have an inner battle with myself to let things go and not over analyse someone's actions. The inner battle has become quieter as I get older and I have gained more self-confidence in my actions and myself.

My over-analysis of those around me lets me read a situation or environment from the smallest of body movements or the way someone says a word. I now use this ability to analyse a situation, then progress personally and professionally. I find it easy to fit into different social occasions, different age groups and from a variety of backgrounds. It is no longer something that hinders me and stops me from involving myself with people, something that makes me become so wrapped up in the situation that I cannot move forward, and doubt every word and action I make.

It is only since I took on responsibility for my younger brother last year that I really started to look at 'what I deserve' when it came to relationships. For many years I have felt lucky to even have someone in my life, but a lot of the time I have put myself and kept myself in negative relationships because I believed I didn't deserve better or didn't really recognise that the relationship was damaging to myself. I am not saying that I have dated men that are horrid, but I have been in situations where I haven't felt confident or comfortable or I've ignored warning signs that things were not right because I haven't wanted to face the truth about certain things.

THE BRIGHTNESS OF STARS

If I were to think about the kind of man I've chosen to be with, I seem to pick people who aren't straightforward; there is always something about them that makes it difficult to be with them - or maybe it's something about me that makes it difficult to be with me. I could analyse myself all day and still not come to a sane conclusion, and I can hear my family and friends saying: "Don't be bloody stupid, it's not you!" I may not have massive faults but I have seemed to get myself into situations that just don't work.

But this is changing. In the past year and a half I became an instant parent to a teenage boy who had lost his dad very suddenly due to cancer and who had never had much contact with his (our) mother. I also graduated from university and started on a career creating journey in terms of work. Needless to say, I have grown up; I have had to use the pain and dysfunctional life I have had both to move forward with work relating to Looked After Children and Care Leavers and also in my personal life. I am able to see the positives and faults of my life, and use them to make sure that my brother gets the best from life. Without having this life experience, I do not think I would be able to handle such responsibilities.

The parental responsibilities I have links to my relationships. I no longer just think about myself when thinking about relationships. I think about what affect it would have on my brother, and if it would be positive to both his and my life. I don't mean I'm looking for a father figure for him; rather I mean the effects of me being happy and stable for my brother.

I do wonder about how my life has changed over the years, and how different it is to a 'normal' life. It has not been an easy ride, but as I mentioned before I would not change anything about it. I believe I have been able to create a positive life for myself despite certain hardships, and who knows, I may have still had a positive life without such things happening but that would be comparing with something that hasn't happened, and I am not one to dwell on 'what if's'. I take a situation and try and get the best from it whatever the circumstances."

*

Chapter Thirteen
Caroline – Resilience

Having worked with young people in all sorts of adverse situations, alongside having lived with many hurting and suffering young people through my adolescent experiences of being in care and also homeless, Caroline's story still had the power to shock. I'm not often shocked. I've seen and heard more than most but she has been through unimaginable things. That is why she has to sit next to the word resilience; not because the rest of us have not developed resilience – of course we have, or we would not be here speaking our stories, using our voices. But because Caroline has overcome unimaginable horrors and become a woman with a business, a relationship, friendships, I felt that it was her word. Her starting point could have taken her to her death, as I'm sure it must have nearly done on many occasions, but instead it took her to a life of her own choosing and making.

re·sil·ience

noun

1. The ability to recover quickly from illness, change, or misfortune; buoyancy.

2. The property of a material that enables it to resume its original shape or position after being bent, stretched, or compressed; elasticity.

*

Caroline's story

"I spent a long time being angry at people for not helping me. I didn't understand why they wouldn't when that was what they were supposed to do. Then one day I realised that it wasn't that they wouldn't, they just couldn't. They had never come across a case like me before, and I didn't know how to tell them what help I needed. I don't think I even knew myself.

In hindsight I can see how challenging it would have been for them. And how different the me they saw was from the me I was inside. They never stood a chance of helping me, which was exactly the point when I was created, I guess. My abusers were very clever in making sure that even if I did ever escape, I wouldn't be able to talk about what happened, or if by some chance I did, I wouldn't be believed.

I remember getting to my first foster home late at night, being shown to this strange room with strange people and just sitting on the bed, knees clutched to my chest, feeling like my whole world had fallen apart. I remember my new 'foster mother' reaching out to touch me and say hello and how I flinched so badly I hit my head on the wall. It had only been two days; I still wasn't used to any touch that wasn't pain.

She was nice, that first foster mother and, given time, I would have been okay there I think, but time is something you don't have in foster care. She was patient with me, didn't get angry at my lack of response, sat with me in my silence. She knew that I was broken and she worked hard to make me feel safe.

In honesty, that first night, all I wanted to do was take it all back, to rewind the clock and go back to the familiar, no matter how painful it was. I had run to save my own life, but not until afterwards, not until the authorities were involved, did I realise that by doing that someone else, most likely my child, would bear my punishment for me. I couldn't stand having any more blood on my hands and I couldn't communicate to them that I had to go back, because they didn't know where I had come from in the first place. So I was trapped in my own internal hell of guilt and fear combined with confusion at this new world I was in. Not to mention that I was very well trained. So whilst I screamed and cried and fought inside, all they were faced with was an empty shell.

I never stood a chance in social services. They don't have the resources to deal with a case like mine. They don't have the time to piece the puzzle together, they don't have the training and, back then at least, I don't think they even knew that people like me existed, at least not in rural Cheshire anyway. And foster carers, no matter how much they tried, just weren't equipped to deal with me, especially not when they usually had 3 or 4 other children to look after too. To be honest it was the other children that made things hardest for me. I couldn't cope with the noise, the unpredictability, the knowledge that I wasn't like them. I needed to be somewhere where it was just me, where I could get my bearings and start understanding the world before having to venture out into it. But as I said, I don't think it even occurred to anyone that this world was new to me. That I might not understand things that other people took as normal. And I didn't know how to communicate my needs to them.

I think if I had been violent or acting out, or even if I had cried, they would have found me easier to deal with. But as it was I was just silent. Not speaking, not sleeping, not eating, not even drinking. So after two weeks they decided I needed to be in a psych ward instead, before I starved to death. I can't blame them for that really. In some ways that was my salvation.

The teenage psychiatric centre was basically a house with 10 residents who supposedly had group therapy and also cooked and cleaned etc. Normally filled with girls with eating disorders, unfortunately for me when I was admitted it housed 9 boys, all of whom were either schizophrenic or manic depressive. I was raped the first day I was there.

In a way that seemed ok because I knew how to cope with being raped. This was familiar. In fact, I wouldn't even call it rape because back then I didn't know I even had a choice. It was the first thing I had understood in a long time though.

My saving grace during my initial time here was one particular nurse, Marilyn, who I fully credit with the fact I am still alive and in any way sane. Somehow she saw me in a way that no one else had, and knew that all I needed was permission. I remember her sitting me down, grabbing my hands so that I couldn't use my usual dissociation technique, holding my chin up so that I looked into her eyes and telling me: "Caroline, you have to drink this water. You have to eat this porridge. You have permission to eat and drink whenever you need now."

It sounds like such a stupid thing, but when you have been programmed, what you need is for someone to communicate with you on that same level your abusers did; it's the only way to get through. In a similar way she gave me permission to speak. It wasn't quite as simple as that, but that's the easiest way to explain it. She broke through the wall and helped me to enter the normal world, a little bit at a time. Within two weeks I was a friendly 14 year old who had discovered a love of both cooking and taking care of people. I was the one who made all the meals, kept the staff fuelled on cups of coffee and who stopped the boys hurting themselves.

I never talked about what had happened to me. As part of our first conversation Marilyn had said to me that she knew my scars were not self-inflicted as everyone else thought, that she knew I was not deliberately anorexic, that my silence was not me being difficult and that I was not clinically depressed. She knew I was scared of the consequences of what I had done, and she knew that I had been raped and treated violently for my whole life. And she told me that she also knew I would never talk to them about it, that this wasn't the time, and that actually they didn't have the resources to deal with what I had to say. She told me to use that place to learn how to take care of myself. So I did.

She probably shouldn't have said all of that. But actually, it was the best thing she could have done. It took all pressure off me to explain my circumstances, and so I could concentrate on simply getting through each day. And I also knew that there was someone who understood the dark place I came from. She also stopped them from ever putting me on medication, for which I will always be very grateful. I was never offered therapy, which in hindsight was a little strange.

My social worker, interestingly enough, didn't like the progress I had made and asked for Marilyn to be removed from my case. I didn't know that initially; I thought Marilyn had given up on me, and that hurt like hell at the time as she was the first person I ever trusted. I felt abandoned and not good enough and for the first time I did cut myself, and promptly became bulimic too.

I was in there for 8 months. After Marilyn left I didn't really make any further progress, but I wasn't in the way, in fact I kept the house running, and social services had nowhere else to put me. I'd learnt by then how to put on a fairly good pretence of normal, and they had quickly decided that despite my obvious difficulties, I was neither psychotic nor depressed.

For the last 6 months I was sent to various foster homes at weekends. The ones I liked, I was quickly moved on from, which never really made sense to me. When I finally left the centre as they needed the bed, I was placed in a home that couldn't be any more inappropriate if it tried. I really don't know why the social worker chose this one over the ones I liked, but she never really seemed to have my best interests at heart to be honest, and out of everyone in the process she is the one who I spent a long time being angry at.

THE BRIGHTNESS OF STARS

I lasted 10 weeks in this foster home, which should never have been allowed to have vulnerable children. I had just turned 15 and on the day my foster father and two of his friends decided to spend an afternoon raping and beating me, I left. I still remember walking three and a half miles with broken ribs, a broken arm, and covered in blood, and not a single person stopping to ask if I was okay or needed help. I don't think I have ever hated people as much as I did that day. When I made it to the hospital and they called social services, I ran. Living on the streets was much more appealing than going back into the system.

I know that my experiences of being in care were not typical, thankfully. The social services department was investigated a year later, and my own social worker fired for misconduct. (Both these investigations were nothing to do with my case, so God knows who else they 'helped' badly.) As far as I know my disappearance was never investigated, and despite me being a ward of state (so they should have had duty of care of me until I was 21) on the two future occasions when I did ask for assistance, I was told that there was no point in them getting involved.

My time in care broke me in a way my previous childhood didn't. Initially I was self-aware enough to know that my childhood was not typical. That the people I grew up with were not even typical of abusers, let alone 'normal' people. So to a certain extent, once the spell had been broken, I was quite prepared to take the world at face value and in some ways was quite naïve and innocent. But the fact that yet more people who were supposed to be taking care of me then let me down and hurt me, confirmed to me what I had been told as a child – that I was evil, just something to be used and hurt and not good for anything else. That I didn't deserve to be in the world and that no one would ever love or care for me. I learnt to hate myself more than I have ever hated any of my abusers, and that the real world was just as cruel as the world I had left; it was just more underhand about it. It taught me not to trust anyone, depend on anyone or ask anyone for help. But it also made me independent.

Had I stayed in care I would be dead now, without a doubt, whether through drink and drugs or the illness that was slowly killing me all that time without anyone knowing. I would never have survived the streets, never have had the resources to get a job and a flat at the age of just 15. I would never have been able to simply walk away and get on a plane to Australia when I was 16, and if I hadn't done that, I wouldn't have begun the journey of healing I have been on for the last 12 years. I would never have realised how much I was capable of and I would never have become determined to educate myself and make my life better. I guess I was broken already; all care did was strengthen the wounds and give me something to fight against."

*

THE BRIGHTNESS OF STARS

Chapter Fourteen
Pav - Integrity

I came by Pav rather accidentally – not that I believe in accidents of this profound nature. Pav is a friend of a friend and I had been spotted on Facebook. The friend who had inadvertently connected us had no idea that Pav, someone he had known for a long time, had a background in care. As a very eloquent, articulate, Oxbridge-educated man he defies stereotypes about what it is to have been a child in care, suffering with adolescent mental health issues more than most. Having 'locked down' his experiences for many years, the writing of his time in care was very hard for him to do although he revealed that he had found a huge weight lifted from him once he had done it and I felt internally very pleased that I had been a part of a cathartic process by default.

in·teg·ri·ty

noun

1. Steadfast adherence to a strict moral or ethical code

2. The state of being unimpaired; soundness

3. The quality or condition of being whole or undivided; completeness

*

Pav's story

"It is strange that I agreed to write about a segment of my life that pre-dates my teenage years just as I am trying to control the breakneck speeds at which I find myself hurtling towards my mid thirties and the impending dawn of middle age. It is stranger still that I agreed to reflect on memories from this period which I have long sought to leave behind – a time about which my mind has seemingly battened down the hatches so effectively that I am still not clear how I escaped the experience so unscathed – on the face of it at least.

A careful review of these times, in the early 1990s, when I lived in the care of a local authority children's home in a run-down corner of Chorley, Lancashire, in North West England, unlocks many clues about the person I was and who I have become. This is to say that I have never really left my care home experience behind. Not entirely. Equally though, I did not leave my care home experience without some of the scrapes presenting me with a set of invaluable life skills and lessons that I have firmly fixed to my arsenal of survival tools. These have proved loyal companions in an overwhelmingly gratifying journey of discovery, disruption as well as personal and professional fulfilment.

To be clear from the outset, and in the framework of the care home graduate's experience, I consider myself a positive case study of what can be achieved with the right support, coupled with a single-minded determination to succeed and prove the detractors wrong.

During my time in care, I learned the valuable lesson that my capacity to succeed – against the odds – must not be limited by the naturally defensive need to survive in spite of the limitations placed upon me. Instead, I learned to embrace my reality with an offensive sense of courage that would allow me to set myself ambitions that most others could not imagine would be possible within the microcosm of my modest universe.

The hallmark to survival for many in my 'home' was rampant substance abuse; predatory emotional and sexual exploitation by external forces who hung around the gates of the 'home' preying on the vulnerability of the occupants within as well as, of course, the unchecked criminality. The casual violence, the misogyny and racism were symptoms of damaged young people calling out for some help and not getting it from those that should have been there, and the substitutes never being enough. Is it any wonder many of us carry scars into our adult lives, even if we learn to live with and mask them as best we can?

I also know that the aggressive racism and exclusion that I experienced during my care home experience helped me to escape exposure to the worst elements because it meant that I could instead turn my attention to books and learning. But even then confusion reigned.

I remember coming across Larkin's poem, This Be the Verse (They fuck you up, your mum and dad...). It was a means to channel my 'anger', only I don't think I had much time to feel anger or grief. I just remember the adrenalin that comes from fear and the need to fight through the grind of a system that spits you out aged 16-18 to fend for yourself.

It would be an almost certain understatement for an outsider looking in at my 'looked after child' prospects to assume that these were nothing if not as grim as the backdrop of Chorley's decaying economy and the socially dysfunctional experiences that characterised much of the community that was my 'home' for more years than I care to remember. Yes, the material hardships were omnipresent: there was no money, there was no support structure to speak of, and there was a heavy emphasis on trying to get me through each day, one at a time, rather than encouraging me to 'waste' my time on the futility of creating a roadmap for a more promising future that was unlikely to be realised. I remember my greatest shock being the profound nihilism and poverty of ambition surrounding me and my prospects. The expectations were so low that it was easy to fall victim to the gloom that was predicted.

How it is possible that all this stands in marked contrast to my present day self: a Cambridge graduate with a Masters degree, the directorship of an international organisation, who spends far too much time in airport lounges and boutique hotels in far away places. In these days when I am preoccupied with tackling issues of labour law and contractual negotiations in private enterprises, living an incredibly privileged and wholesome life, it still confounds me that I used to worry about how much food I should store away in my bedside cabinet – because it was difficult to know when I might get my next meal, if I had enough money to buy provisions for the week ahead, while the innocuous-sounding 'Independence Training Unit' I inhabited was overrun by care home bullies inflicting assault after assault on me under the partial gaze of in-house supervisors. There were no such things as corporate parents in those days so there was a clear disconnect between the people the policy makers were making decisions about.

Given all this, it stands to reason that the realisation that I could achieve more was not immediately obvious to me during my early stages of being institutionalised. No one dared to lift my expectations in case they might have to follow it through with some sort of support or action plan. Part of me wants to be scathing about the lack of social support but I don't feel capable of this because it was also a gradual journey towards seeking a sense of self-identity and self-value during these dark times.

Being subjected to gratuitous and brutal knocks from being a solitary, non-white child in a care home where one's peers were determined to project their understandably misguided anger on the person who least fit, and had the fewest allies in a modestly complex web of care home social constructs and political hierarchies, served its purpose. When I reflect back, it was almost inevitable that I would respond to this injustice with a long-term commitment to challenging bigotry and prejudice. The experience also left me averse to operations which require a pack mentality, where blind and unquestioning loyalty to a cause has to be refracted through a tribal responsibility that might trump the actual interests of real communities of people. The need to do what was right, rather than what was expected, has held strong within me, even when it has proved to be the less popular choice to make. It has not always made me friends, but it has emboldened me to speak up and to make the case for what I see and think without being bound by dogma.

In this sense, I still feel a little surprised that I have managed to survive and have flourished both privately and professionally. Recognition of success ought not to be mistaken for arrogance or conceit. It is not. When you have walked in my shoes, which have not always been my own, and you have witnessed the things that I have seen, which have not always been my choice or in my interest, then you can allow yourself some flexibility to arrive at a point where you can validate your own achievements and experiences on terms that you define, regardless of what others think. Naturally, this creates a paradoxical situation for others, when they are without any sense of the journey I have undertaken, they can perceive me as a precocious, Oxbridge-educated prima donna, rolling in privilege. I recognise their assumptions because I occupy shades of all those things but I know there is more to it.

In his seminal work, A Man of the People, the Nigerian author and academic, Chinua Achebe, asked: 'What is modesty but inverted pride?' I was 19 years old when I embraced this challenge to be honest about my successes – as much as I seek to be honest about my failures – because it would be disingenuous not to acknowledge the hallmark of my transition from care home experience to where I am now: a place where I share the highs and lows of other 'normal' people, as a place that is deeply connected to my ability to validate and accept the challenges that I have overcome. This is not self-indulgent narcissism. It is a pragmatic coming to terms with the cards life has dealt me and the fact that I have learned to play those cards to the best of my ability. It is connected to the perseverance I have shown in the face of tests that might have broken others.

At my most pugnacious I might argue that the palpable, outward self-confidence and self-belief I exude comes from having successfully jumped through the hoops and passed the tests that society set for me. Conversely, it is intrinsically connected to the contradictory and strategic amnesia that I have had to employ throughout my adolescent and adult life. Just as it was when I was living in institutionalised care – that I was largely out of sight and out of mind – for a long time I have sought to manage this and subsequent traumatic experiences by ignoring them as far as possible. It means that I have earned the right to be the way I am which, ironically, masks the person that I privately most identify with: a troubled teen with immense insecurities who needs to learn to trust others despite being a thoroughbred survivor who no one can really hurt because the damage has all been done.

Perhaps this is one reason why I have not actively sought to fully reconcile my experiences that rest among the emotional and psychological debris that has littered my life. They spike me like the small and corrosive shards of metal that indiscriminately pierce the flesh after a high-impact cluster bomb hits the ground among dense urban populations. If the wounds from my care home experience had been allowed to fester they would have risked depriving my spirit of the oxygen that was important to both heal and build resistance to other infections. Had I not bound my wounds up and sought safety through reading and self-education then I may not have survived the experience or fulfilled anywhere near my potential.

In another of his essays, The Education of a British-Protected Child, Chinua Achebe writes that to answer oppression with appropriate resistance requires knowledge of two types: in the first place, self-knowledge by the victim, which is to say that one must be aware that oppression exists, and an awareness that the victim has fallen from a great height of promise into the present depths. Achebe also argues that the victim must know who the enemy is. He must know his oppressor's real name, not an alias, a pseudonym, or a nom de plume.

The reason that Achebe's work will always stay with me is not only because he strongly influenced my personal philosophy of speaking truth to power, no matter how painful that experience must be, but his work also emboldened me to confront my oppressor – fear of dependency and failure – with a sense of permission to speak out about the things that I know too well.

As many children who have been in care will know about directly, or indirectly, from their own experiences, when you are engaged in a jihad – a personal struggle – for your very spiritual and physical survival, without a blueprint or roadmap to direct you, then you quickly learn that self-reliance and self-sufficiency are your greatest assets. The sooner you realise this the sooner it bears fruit in an otherwise traumatic episode in your life.

While the physical body experiences trauma that can be seen upon its flesh, as wounds that can be seen and rationalised, they can often be left to heal themselves or with modest clinical intervention. But when the soul is subjected to suffering that is often unspoken and invisible, it can remain with you for a lifetime. That pain is dulled with time as you learn to adapt but it does not go away. Not really. Not ever.

The decision to revisit old ground has been predicated as much by happening across others who, like me, have successfully transitioned from being a 'looked after child' in a local authority care home to 'active citizens' in the mainstream of society, as much as a sense that it is time to speak out.

It is no surprise to me that I managed to get very good A Level grades and went on to Cambridge despite the underlying suffering that has rarely been given a voice. It was what convention demands. But in these times of supposedly 'shocking' revelations about people in positions of power, from politicians in government circles to celebrities in cultural institutions, right the way across the spectrum to localised actors engaged in 'extraordinary' acts of organised grooming, that exploit and violate the most vulnerable, I feel it is time to say that I want to be done with hurting and hiding. I want to be done with excusing or proving. I owe my benefactors everything. I owe my detractors nothing.

And at this time when those who wield institutional power, from MPs to the media, are engaged in shrill headline-grabbing tirades about the fact that 'child protection systems fail to listen' to teenagers' voices, at a time when the economic and educational prospects of an entire generation of working class young people is being decimated, I find myself asking: what is new? How is this different to how it has always been?

For sure, some things have gotten better, but the voice of young people has always been suppressed or muted. Not because they have nothing to say but more because the resources that would be required to act on their calls are not what policymakers are prepared to invest in.

The Victorian model of tough experiences making young people strong and sturdy is completely obliterated among young people with different attitudes and values towards work and life. After all, the new generation of young people tend to be socially and environmentally conscious because their life events have been shaped by the economic crisis, global warming, globalization, and the digital revolution. The new forms of technologies and communication that are available have made their experience increasingly global.

And still, despite an abundance of indicators for success to reassure me, I have continued to struggle to find the voice to be able to tell my story about being in care on such candid terms that society might be ready to face up to what happens to looked after children, or how we – in society – so readily allow young people to slip out of the mainstream and face almost certain calamity in their personal and professional lives.

Throughout life I have learned that I do not like suffering to no purpose. I feel that suffering should give birth to something good and creative. So I do not blame anyone. I do not pity or regret my experiences: but I do struggle to get a grip with how I got through things so unscathed. What I'm certain of is that none of it would have been possible without my teachers, my siblings and – unfashionable as it may be to admit – my faith in God, who was often the only 'friend' I could always turn to in good times and bad.

I have long sought to convince myself that I am free from the effects of my pre-, mid- and post-care experiences, but I know I am still haunted by them. I want to say that I've moved on and I keep telling myself that I have done so, but coming back to the subject reminds me that I have not and I know that I still genuinely fear: my past and my present, and possibly even my future too. As Achebe reminds us, in order to answer oppression with appropriate resistance we must have knowledge, and we must name the oppressor. Fear.

I still experience nightmares about having to sit an A Level French written exam. I often thought this fear was connected to the anxiety that exams naturally provoke in many people, but I actually know – in my subconscious – that this is not the case. If fact be known, I was hospitalised in a psychiatric ward around the time of my A Level exams and my body was being pumped full of chemicals that harmed me. I recall scenes of my sister weeping at my bedside as she visited me. I remember her asking me to fight what I was battling in my mind and to pull through. Even now, I bite my lip and hold back tears as I recall the tears running down my own face as I sat in my hospital chair facing the fear that I knew myself but I was losing myself. I remember wanting to cry out but the medication had seen to it that my voice was muted. The powerful drugs they pump into patients put paid to any heroic act of resistance that Achebe writes about. I could not break the cycle of powerlessness and destruction that I was living and I was not being enabled by the 'system'.

One way or another, I managed to get through this experience of mental ill-health. In a manner that has been characteristic of my care home graduate experience, I have learned how to mask my inner turmoil with an external air of serenity. I have learned to perfect the suppression of what happens within in pursuit of a socially and culturally normative facade.

I compare this experience to the poem, 'The Second Coming' by the Irish poet William B. Yeats who, in the aftermath of the First World War, used religious imagery about the Apocalypse and second coming as allegory to describe the atmosphere in post-war Europe. What Yeats described as the "rough beast" slouching towards Bethlehem was the symbol of a new age, while the speaker's vision of a rising sphinx was his vision of the character of the new world.

In my internal world war, I felt Yeats captured the contrary forces at work in my own history, about the conflict between the experiences I had left behind, the world I inhabited, and the uncertain future that lay before me. Knowing as we do the trauma of the Second World War, Yeats' prophesising was not entirely off the mark as an allegory to my life, in relation to my struggle to reinvent myself and grow in the face of uncertainty and the absence of cultural capital and economic means.

Over these past months of confronting the fact that I have, in my own small way, reinvented the cycle described in Yeats' poetry, it has been a reminder that despite the 'success' and stability – which is both real and laboured – there is what might best be expressed as my Freudian id's conflicting struggle with my Freudian ego's efforts to suppress in order to make me conform. On the whole, my ego has managed to contain my id successfully and I have constructed a relatively solid and stable manifestation of myself to the world I inhabit. This has enabled me to make social and professional progress.

In life, from my care home to the present, I have learned that individuals derive strength from their society, and societies derive strength from the individuals who belong to them. I feel like I have built my cultural capital, social fortune and strength with the help of my societies' customs. Equally, I hope that the societies I have inhabited have benefited somewhat from my hard work and determination – despite the starting point from which I originated."

*

THE BRIGHTNESS OF STARS

Chapter Fifteen
Siani - Visibility

Siani had found her way onto the Author page on my website and wrote to me with her story. While it wasn't quite what I was looking for for the book, the relevance of it seemed obvious so we began our discussions.

To have been where she was at the particular time that she was there, with the national media pointing cameras in her direction, and to not be found is an irony too painful to bear. To be so invisible could only create a vibrancy that would ensure visibility.

vis·i·bil·i·ty

noun

1. The fact, state, or degree of being visible.

2. The greatest distance under given weather conditions to which it is possible to see without instrumental assistance.

3. a. The capability of being easily observed: an executive with high visibility.

b. The capability of providing a clear, unobstructed view: a windshield with good visibility.

*

So this last story is of the only person I chose who has not been in care. Given that this book is completely focused on the stories of adults who have been in care, you might wonder where Siani fits in.

Siani contacted me initially to share her story and her recovery from years of abuse and to tell me that she was now happily married and working with children for a well-known charity. I was keen to have her in this book from the outset and then discovered that she hadn't been in care.

As her story unfolded, it became more and more relevant, I'm sure you'll agree, because Siani lived on the Orkney Islands at the time of the huge scandal where social workers mistakenly removed nine children from their families. It was February 1991 and the raids saw five boys and four girls, aged 8 to 15 and all from the families of English 'incomers', taken into care. This raid was a response to talk of ritualistic satanic abuse by a girl from an island family during therapy sessions with social workers and police. What unfolded on tiny South Ronaldsay in Orkney that morning in early 1991 triggered Scotland's biggest case of alleged satanic child abuse. Although the allegations were eventually dismissed and ridiculed as completely false, it still remains known as the Orkney child abuse scandal.

While all of this activity, this huge investigation carried out under the intense focus on the protection of children, was taking place on a tiny 'no place to hide' island, no one came for Siani. No one questioned a thing and as her story unfolds, the painful irony of it all won't fail to leave you bewildered.

*

Siani's Story

"I've never actually been in care. There have been times, however, over the years, when I wished I was. I was brought up on a remote Scottish island, with unconventional parents – my father was 30 years older than my mother, and had been her teacher at school. After they met, they soon moved from the Midlands to Scotland, partly to escape the stigma they faced as a couple with a large age gap. My father had been married three times before, and had himself experienced a traumatic and abusive childhood. I believe that this led to him developing a physically and emotionally abusive personality, which spilled over into his marriages and his parenting – he already had four children by the time he met my mum.

I can see WHY he was the way he was – he was born in 1928 and in his era, you didn't talk about family problems, abuse, children's rights. If you were getting beaten (as he was) it didn't get flagged up at all. Nor could you talk about your trauma later in life – if you admitted to struggling with mental health issues, it was likely you would be medicated or institutionalised. So my father kept his problems to himself, suffering from terrible depression and rages, passing on the violence he suffered as a child to his wives and children.

As a child, I did live in fear of him. My mum was also quite slap-happy, but her behaviour paled in comparison to his. From literally my first memory, all I can recollect is fear, hiding, guilt, pain and anxiety, as he controlled everything about our lives. He regularly fell into terrifying rages which led to beatings and screaming and shouting that could last for days. As we all tiptoed around him in fear he would decide his current black mood was down to one of us – which it generally was. We could only eat certain foods, we weren't allowed to watch telly or listen to any radio apart from local radio or Radio 4.

We didn't attend school – we were all home educated, which meant the only interaction we had with the local authorities was the annual check by the council education officers, who would drink tea and look at our schoolwork, which was impeccable – they never queried our lack of social interaction or unusually quiet politeness to strangers. As well as the lack of social interaction, we were physically quite isolated – we didn't often mix with other children, and when my parents' friends came over, things were all sweetness and light – he never lost his temper in front of anyone else. I felt sorry for my mum, but at the same time I was very angry with her for putting up with him and not standing up to him. The way she intervened when he was beating my brother, for example, was not to stop him, but to rescue his spectacles in case they got broken – we couldn't afford new ones. It was the same when she sat at the doctor's and said that the goat had knocked her over, after he'd pushed her and she'd fallen, breaking her wrist. She was obviously scared of him, cried a lot of the time, and didn't know what to do. She was very young (she had four of us before her 30th birthday) and inexperienced, having left school and run away with him at 16.

When I was eight years old, a scandal befell the island. A group of families were accused of satanic sexual abuse of children, and several children were abducted from their homes in a dawn raid by Social Services. This was in the days before you had to have reams of evidence before you could remove a child, and they literally took the children on rumour and hearsay. They were absent for months, during which time the island was split into camps of campaigners trying to get them back, and the rest who believed 'there's no smoke without fire'. As it turned out, the accusations were entirely fabricated and eventually the children were returned and many social workers lost their jobs.

However, in the meantime, my father went a bit crazy. He became obsessed with the idea that because we knew one of the families whose children had been taken, we would be taken ourselves, and I imagine he was worried about what we would say if we WERE interviewed. So he did what every crazy paranoid abusive parent would do – he sent us 'on the run' for over a month. We left the island on a ferry and took a coach all the way to London, to stay with various relatives. I remember little of the trip, apart from a lot of crying and being ill – for some reason I was sick a lot – and I refused to take my hat off, which was odd because my brother refused to take his shoes off. In retrospect, we were all really terrified because we'd been led to believe we could be stolen away by some evil social workers, so we were both hiding and ready to flee.

While we were away, my father enjoyed the notoriety he received from sending us away – he was a very intelligent man (he's got a PhD and has published books) and he was very convincing in his role of indignant father having sent away his children to protect them (as opposed to the truth – a scared abuser who might be found out). Eventually we went home and the other families were reunited with their children, and the whole thing died down – but things didn't get any easier with our father; he remained as bad, if not worse than before.

As I grew up, his temper remained and although he hit out less towards me, his behaviour towards my two little brothers filled me with anger. I used to lie with my ear to the floor of my bedroom, trying to hear what was going on as he ranted and raged, praying that my mum and brothers would be ok. I was filled with terrible hatred towards him, and fantasised about running down the stairs and stabbing him, and in my fantasy my family would be overjoyed about being freed from him and we'd hide the body and we would all live happily ever after.

The lack of outside intervention in our lives was something that didn't really occur to me until later. The local council never checked up on us apart from that annual visit, and doctors seemed unconcerned. Our nearest neighbour said to my mum one day, "How is Peter, is he ill? We've not heard him shouting in days!" If your neighbour shouted so often you noticed when he hadn't, would you not think to tell someone?! Literally nobody said or did anything. Not my mother, the council, the doctors, neighbours. Nobody.

When I was fifteen, I began to rebel – cutting my hair, piercing myself, developing strange habits like stealing food and pretending to find money in the street that I had in fact stolen from my mum's handbag. I developed a strange relationship with food, which led to a lot of comfort eating and weight gain that I have only resolved in the last two years! I can now see that all this behaviour was symptomatic of a very troubled youth. I met an older man, a friend of a man who used to babysit us when we were very young. This older man befriended me and, lacking any love or understanding, I easily fell under his spell. To cut a long story short, he groomed me for many months before sexually assaulting me, all under the guise of providing a caring, listening ear. Shortly after the assault, he left the island and was never seen again. And again, nobody cared or even noticed what was happening.

I left home at 16. I found a boyfriend who was a little older, a harmless kind man who was the first person to treat me nicely. We spent the summer travelling around the country in a car, camping and working at festivals. I met lots of very kind and spiritual people, and began to see how the world worked.

But the pattern of being around an abusive man was not broken. After a couple of years with this nice man, I met a dangerous guy. He was ten years older, a traveller, and a carbon copy of my father: controlling, abusive and manipulative. I foolishly left the nice guy and ran off with the nasty one, living on a travellers' site for a few years, in a caravan, in fear.

Again, I found myself living in terror – not allowed to wear makeup, cut my hair, wear tight clothes, go to the doctor or dentist, drink. You might think it ridiculous for an 18 year old woman to succumb to such treatment, but as anyone who has been through parental abuse will know, the pattern was just repeating itself. This man never actually hit me, but would destroy my belongings, throw things at me, stab knives in the wall above my head if I sniffed too loudly, self-harm and blame it on me, shout, rant, rage and threaten to kill me if I left.

Again nobody intervened. The difference between this situation and the one involving my father was that more people were aware of what was going on and still didn't do anything. That was, until I moved to a travellers' site in the Midlands, and met a bunch of decent people. One of them gave me the courage to change things. I knew that if I tried to leave him when he was present I could end up dead, so I waited until he was 100 miles away visiting friends, and called him.

I was strong, firm, and stuck to my guns, and by the time he made it back I had bought my own caravan at the opposite end of the field and moved all my belongings into it – and had the whole of the site's residents keeping an eye on me to make sure I was ok. Over the years he's tried to get me back, and once I left the site he tried to find me, but to no avail. After a few years, he met another vulnerable young woman and abused and manipulated her, getting her pregnant. One day I had a call from an old friend. He was with this girl, who was growing in realisation about the guy, and she wanted to talk to me. I am so glad she reached out to me, because I could do what that friend had done to me, and be the person to tell her she could choose a different path. She left with her baby before he could hurt her any more (he had graduated to setting fire to her caravan and pushing her over with the baby) and she is now on her own, independent and strong, and a great mum.

Around seven years after I left home, just after I'd escaped the abusive boyfriend, the growing realisation of everything that had happened began to sink in. I became extremely depressed, suffered from terrible anxiety and sank into a deep, dark place. Once I started having panic attacks, nightmares, flashbacks, I realised it might be time to see a doctor. I was put on antidepressants and the waiting list for some counselling. The counselling was scary, but wonderful – I was lucky to have a very good counsellor who gave me the tools to move forward and begin my journey to recovery. I realised that a rewarding job would help me emotionally, and I worked hard to get a job in a nursery with pre-schoolers. I was determined to change the past and ensure I didn't pass on the trauma to the next generation. After a year, I decided I was ok to come off the antidepressants, so did so – without any advice to wean off, I just stopped dead. This was a BIG mistake, as my emotions went haywire and I went into a spiral of craziness! However, I was determined that to beat my demons, I had to grow the strength within myself rather than relying on meds. At this time, I had a really dark moment – I found myself standing by my bathroom window, crying, with a craft knife pressed against my wrist. As they sometimes say, you have to hit rock bottom before you can climb back up. I realised I had a choice – give in, or ask for help. I texted a very good friend who knew some of what I had been through, and within two hours, he was on my doorstep with chocolate and an order: "That's it, you're moving to Worcester so I can keep an eye on you!!"

I moved to Worcester and met a circle of wonderful friends. I got another job in a nursery and started doing an NVQ in childcare. I took one day at a time, and I started to talk about everything that had happened to me. I talked about it all with good friends who had been through similar things. I changed jobs – I started working in a special school, with some kids who had been in care or adopted. I saw their pain and began to help them to see there was a different way to be – they didn't have to follow the path that was set out for them.

I read – a LOT. I read about others who had suffered, and I read self-help books on changing your path. (Two of these books are John Bradshaw's Homecoming, and Dale Carnegie's How to Stop Worrying and Start Living). Very gradually, my strength grew. I went to university and got a 2:1 degree in Education with Learning Support – I studied modules on child development, SEN, emotional and behavioural difficulties, children in care, disaffected youth, social studies. These studies helped to inform the basis for my growth, as I realised that I was RIGHT – what had happened to me WAS wrong! People SHOULD have helped!

This knowledge didn't cause me to carry resentment; on the contrary, I felt relieved as my beliefs were reaffirmed by my growing knowledge. I determined NOT to repeat my history. And I grew happier. As I grew happier, I grew more and more resilient and conscious of the beauty of life. I became brave and strong, and I wrote to my father, voicing my anger and sorrow. I spoke to my mother, and voiced my resentment and regret. Both of them apologised; my mother cried, my father wrote to me. A weight lifted, and I realised that I could have held onto the anger forever, but instead I chose to let it go.

Doing the job I do now, working in a children's charity, I realise that my experiences have been a positive force. I am strong, empathetic, understanding and tolerant to a different degree to someone who has never experienced the trauma I have. I am fiercely socially responsible, and have stepped in during fights to stop them, given first aid to a fitting heroin addict, called the police when I saw a man chase a woman down the street and drag her into a house. I've called Social Services when I've found out about children being neglected. I'm an interfering pain in the ass of Bad Things, and a fierce champion of Good. And if I hadn't been in the middle of Bad Things, and left alone by the world, I wouldn't know what it was like, and I quite possibly would turn away, not see, not hear, choose to close my mind to the abuse, the fights, the neglect and the pain that was happening under my nose.

Experiences shape a person, yes. They can affect you and drive you into the depths of despair and depression. But I always remember I have a choice: a choice to sink, or pull myself up, grow, and thrive. I can't imagine how hard it must be growing up in care, and I don't know how my life might have turned out differently if I had. As it is, I don't regret a single day of my life because it has led me to this point, right here, writing this. I have a job I love. I'm married to a wonderful man. We're trying for a baby. I've got a group of bloody wonderful friends who I love dearly. I've got three cats, two geckos and an allotment. I'm no longer controlled by food. I have a big, weird, wonderful family, and have forgiven my parents. And I have the knowledge that I have been through a ton of shit, and survived.

Not only have I survived, but I have thrived, grown and learned much on the journey. I'm now in a position to be able to offer advice and guidance to others who are struggling, and if the trauma I went through has enabled me to do that, then surely it was a worthy trial? After all, that is why I believe we are here – to be happy and try to make others happy. Life is joy. And, to use a crude metaphor, a piece of carbon is ground around under the earth for a hell of a long time before it turns into a diamond. And the longer it takes, the brighter the sparkle."

*

Conclusion

When I started to embark upon the journey of this book, the whole exercise was to share lost and unheard voices. I wanted to open up a discussion, to provide some thought-provoking information for foster carers, teachers and staff in social care working directly with young people but essentially, it's been an act of cathartic release for me. I wanted to highlight the strangeness of there being no information in the public domain about the adults who had been children in a system that had been their corporate parent.

While I have been working on this book, life has happened and the landscape has changed a little. The public unveiling of the Jimmy Savile enquiry has altered many things. NSPCC director of child protection advice and awareness Peter Watt said: "The sheer scale of Savile's abuse over six decades simply beggars belief. He is without doubt one of the most prolific sex offenders we have ever come across and every number represents a victim that will never get justice now he is dead." Known to have actively targeted children in care, (among many other vulnerable children) he has, from the grave, placed in the media spotlight the vulnerability of children in care who have been abused by people in power.

The busy media climate of interest in vulnerable children is a frenzy that has a uniqueness about it. Those of us who have been in care, and many who have worked in care, have known for years about the targeted abuse of vulnerable children. It's just that now this knowledge is out in the open, so to speak - on the table, all over the press. The sheer volume of abuse has meant that the public can connect with what is being said. While 99% of the population cannot connect with the experience of being in care, people can create an emotional connection with being in hospital, for example (another one of Savile's favourite places for him to abuse the vulnerable.) Maybe they were in hospital as a child or they have a child who has been in hospital – there is a point of reference. When people make an emotional connection to something, there is an emotional response which means that there is an engagement in the debate from a far wider and more far reaching audience than ever before.

This 'new' climate of knowledge around abuse and vulnerable children means that there is a very real window of opportunity for change. And while I have observed a certain amount of cynicism from some quarters who see this as part of the cycle of noise that will eventually go quiet, I am choosing to believe that this is not the case. Firstly, I am hopeful because I am an eternal optimist but more importantly, I am hopeful that change is coming because we live in a very different world of communication and awareness than we ever have before and this can only be a useful positive thing in relation to improving the protection of vulnerable children.

Maybe, just maybe, children will start to be protected in the way that they should have been from the outset - particularly when a number of those children arriving into the system do so on the back of already having been neglected and abused.

*

One of the things that has made the stories here so compelling is that I am often the first person to whom their story has been told in its entirety. I have had this said to me over and over again and it's an honourable and humbling position to be in. It's not necessarily that people haven't shared their story before but it will have been in bite size chunks with little bits offered to different people at different times. This is much the way that I have told my own story over the years: a manageable collection of painless short stories rather than a gripping emotionally torturous novel.

I think I wanted to understand some of my inner world by seeing if I could find any similarities with other people and on occasion it was like looking in the mirror. The conversations about identity and loss and aloneness and boundaries just rang through me like church bell practice early on a Sunday morning, and they were always spoken by people with whom I really only had 'being in care' as a shared experience. The differences in everyone's stories - and those of anyone who I have ever worked with in a professional capacity - are always so diverse but the similarities ring out as though we were from the same family, in the strangest possible way.

So in my own reflection what first really struck me was that the silence that I lived with during my twenties and thirties was also a shared experience. And I must add that it was not necessarily a deliberate silence - not all the time, at least - but that being a member of only 1% of the population, the power of re-invention of the self and the fact that very few opportunities ever came up to discuss that part of my life meant that these things were often not spoken of. Whereas people talk about their families all the time, people who have been in care don't tend to talk about being in care. The point of reference isn't there. This has meant that some of the people in the book have friends who are not aware of their background.

Having said that, when I work with young people who are in care now, there is a much better mix of privacy and openness, which may be reflective of the times we live in or it may just be that the distance from the system isn't there yet so the young people are still in a more shared environment with others in the same situation.

The other shocking similarity that needs to be highlighted (as if it wasn't being highlighted enough in the media) is that most of the people that I have met who have been in care have at some time experienced abuse, sat next to abuse or comforted someone who has been abused during their time there. There are many things that adults who have been in care do not speak of, but to the trained/experienced eye, we know, we understand and we 'see' what a person describing their time in care has experienced/is aware of. There are many details that are eliminated in this story telling process and I'm sure you understand why. We fill our lives with children, jobs, friends; there are things that don't need to be said explicitly but unfortunately are implicit in the experiences of many people.

And finally, one of the great bonuses for me and a few of the other people that I spoke with for this book has been recognising why I have such a developed sense of justice and inclusion. Living in children's homes is a little like being in Heathrow Airport; it's a little piece of the whole of the world. All cultures, religions, disabilities and abilities living together in one space. Being homeless was no different. I shared spaces with people from every region of the land. I expected, embraced, valued and was comforted by difference, long before it was written down in some sort of Policy and Procedure. It was my 'normal'.

Jane explained this through saying: "I didn't see difference. I didn't feel the difference. We were all just in care." And Noel talked of a "colour blindness" that he felt had come from being a black child in a white family. This backdrop of diversity can have the potential for qualities such as compassion, understanding, tolerance and acceptance; a very positive outcome for care experienced people.

So in conclusion, the positives and negatives sit uneasily side by side, encouraging some personalities to thrive and flourish, others to spend a lifetime searching for answers and others again struggling to be who they might have been had life not dealt them this particular hand of cards.

I therefore believe that young people who come into care have to have the Very Best Parenting, Parenting Extraordinaire if you like. There has to be a chance that those who will flounder without a sense of belonging, or are at risk of predators, or are unable to meet the demands of a constantly changing education system, learn to develop other tools and strategies to have the best chance of flourishing. Good Enough parenting for these children is not good enough.

The development and nurture of social and support networks that encourage long lasting friendships and foster a sense of belonging also have to be integral in the Very Best Parenting approach. My dissertation for my degree all those years ago had been about the lack of support networks provided for young people in care and the effects of that upon self-esteem. Constant house/school moves, poor self-image, shame regarding circumstances and a desire for reinvention are some of the reasons why young people can be and feel so isolated from other young people. Creating spaces where young people can develop friendships and have shared experiences is integral to the work that I do. Watching those connections form by running groups with other local young people is a wonderful thing.

The most astounding feature of the personality of the care experienced has to be awarded to resilience. It is a skill rather than a trait, carried by those who have had to deal with a lot more than most, and it is this that underpins their ability to keep on going, keep on getting up again and keep on striving.

Earlier I mentioned a bag of tools that we can give young people to enable them a smoother transition into adulthood, to better equip them to deal with their experiences of being in care, what brought them there and what experiences they might have afterwards as a direct result of having been in care. This is why I developed a programme of intervention and prevention with the focus on Personal Development. So what do I mean by personal development?

At the level of the individual, personal development includes the following activities:

- o improving self-awareness
- o improving self-knowledge
- o building or renewing identity
- o developing strengths or talents
- o improving wealth
- o spiritual development
- o identifying or improving potential
- o building employability or human capital
- o enhancing lifestyle or the quality of life
- o improving health
- o fulfilling aspirations
- o initiating a life enterprise or personal autonomy
- o defining and executing personal development plans
- o improving social abilities
- o growing resilience

My own personal experience is that I was lucky. I was very lucky. At around my late teens and very early twenties, the doors that had been shut tight were forced open by an alcohol problem that I didn't want to have and my arrival in a life of sobriety a day at a time. This happened to coincide with me being funded to go to university. Every emotional, educational and personal door opened and I was like a sponge. I wanted to learn everything I could about how to build up the mess that I felt I was and how to learn all that I could about my chosen subject.

I was studying Sociology in a university that I thought had made some terrible mistake by allowing me to attend having never written a proper essay before. I had scraped through a couple of

A Levels at a college in a part-drunken, part-sober stupor and here I was, now doing a degree.

Looking back, I now realise that this was a window of opportunity and one that I'm not sure stays continually open without daily work and acknowledgment of it. I asked a few of the contributors their thoughts on this. They all said that there was a period in their lives when they had become "open" to personal development learning and some of them took it, like I did, without even knowing it. Others missed that window of opportunity and had to wait another 20 years for the window to open again.

That is why I believe that the time for intervention is during that all important transition into adulthood, before decisions are made that can affect an entire lifetime. There are some important messages in this book that I hope will provide some new thinking - swiftly followed by those that can taking action.

"In any situation, the best thing you can do is the right thing; the next best thing you can do is the wrong thing; the worst thing you do is nothing."

Theodore Roosevelt

THE BRIGHTNESS OF STARS

Appendix

The Fluffy Dandelion

I run workshops for people wanting to write, whether it's to get published, to find healing or to release a creative burst of writing. I have a secret Facebook group which I provide as part of the on-going support after the workshop, and I set the group members a challenge. I wanted them to write about a dandelion when it's in the fluffy stage, as I felt that there was a connection between the process that the dandelion goes through and something I could recognise in myself and in others through healing and recovery. Isabel took up the challenge and this is what she wrote.

"Sitting alone in a sea of green that is the lawn, a single dandelion is busy preparing for the next stage of its life. Faded is the vivid yellow of its youth. That vibrant sunshiny colour was the bane of the gardener, who toiled in vain to rid his pride and joy, the lawn, of this plant he considered a weed. All of the other dandelions had succumbed to the treatments and had wilted away; this one alone had survived. It was now down to this solitary dandelion to carry on the fight for survival of its species.

One by one, the fluffy little tendrils that would carry the seeds emerged from their resting place and reached up to the light. All that was needed now was for a puff of wind to carry them off on their journey. To start again the miracle of life that all living things have in common. The air on this particular day was very still but patiently they waited, knowing that it was only a matter of time. Suddenly there was the sound of footsteps and the shrill laughter of a child. On seeing the dandelion the child bent down, picked it up and, taking an enormously large breath for a little one, blew the dandelion with all her might. One o'clock, puff, two o'clock, another puff, three o'clock and in three childish breaths the dandelion seeds were sent hurtling through the air.

THE BRIGHTNESS OF STARS

The root of the parent dandelion sighed in satisfaction and settled down to rest until it was time once again to emerge and join the fight to survive the gardener's best efforts. As for the fluffy dandelions, some fell on other lawns and were destined to carry on the fight for survival. Others landed in meadows where all things wild were nurtured and encouraged to bloom. Many found themselves in shady corners hidden away from the prying eyes of men. Destined to live out their existence, unobserved and free, to quietly carry on perpetuating the dandelion species. They might not be noticed but in the future their seeds would, like them, be carried off on the wind and land on a lawn - perhaps even returning to the original home of the solitary dandelion."

Isabel Johnstone 2013

About the Author

Workshop Leader ~ Coffee Snob ~ Mother of Teens ~ Keynote Speaker ~ Author ~ Mentor

After a long career in social work and education, Lisa finally left it all behind her to run her own business, setting up (with a good friend) and running a networking organisation for women and a holistic health practice. In 2011, after blogging happily for a couple of years, Lisa decided to write her first book, Soul Journey, and her world flipped upside down and the pen could not be put down.

An international blogger, published author and writers' workshop leader, Lisa Cherry helps beginner writers to remove the emotional blocks that may be preventing them from starting on writing projects. Lisa works to rebuild confidence that may have diminished over time, helping people arrive at the comfortable place where they can say "I am a writer!"' Lisa provides one-to-one book mentoring/coaching, helps budding authors build their 'platform' (marketing) and runs national programmes for young people who are or have been in care, working with them to help them make sense of their experiences through the written word and develop abilities to express emotional hurt in a safe, positive and growing way.

Lisa is invited to speak regularly in the UK and in Europe to university students, writers' groups, business networking events, conferences and women's groups and has been described as an engaging, inspiring and thought-provoking speaker.

www.lisacherry.co.uk

www.whateveryouthcoaching.co.uk

Email: lisa@lisacherry.co.uk

Twitter: @_lisacherry

Facebook: www.facebook.com/lisacherry.author

Contributors

Carrie

Carrie currently works within the looked after children and care leaver area, and is continuing in her political aim to create positive changes to the outcomes of this cohort. You can contact her via twitter @CWilson200 and her blog is:

carriewilsoncareleaver.blogspot.co.uk/

Caroline

Caroline now lives in the South west of England with her partner and cat. She describes herself as someone who "runs my own business, despite suffering all sorts of severe health problems as a result of my childhood."

Dianne

Dianne has now been happily married for 30 years. She has two sons and lives in Sussex with her husband and their dogs.

Over the last 14 years she has studied and then practised nutritional therapy and NLP. Those years gave birth to her passion for helping people understand how to eat well and why.

Dianne felt galvanised to demystify the arena of healthy eating, making it doable and accessible for everyone. She wanted to reach a wider audience helping those who really need it so now she is a professional blogger, sharing healthy eating wisdom through her website, classes and coaching.

www.healthy-eating.org.uk

Jane

After many years of teaching women returners to education (she taught many women assertiveness skills and Women's Studies on an Access to Higher Education course in a further education college) she now works as a national officer for a teaching trade union. She ensured both her children went through university and both are now successful in their own fields. As a trained counsellor Jane continues to support other women in a voluntary capacity, specialising in working with victims of domestic violence and abuse. Jane continues her own journey to personal fulfilment and growth, but is now happier and more content than at any other time in her life.

Pav

Pav is an experienced trade union employment and equality law practitioner. He is Director for Professionals and Managers at UNI Global Union in Switzerland, having previously worked as Director of Communications at Education International in Belgium, and National Race Equality Officer at UNISON in the UK. Pav's career has also included senior civil service posts within the UK's Department for Education and Department for International Aid.

Since graduating from Cambridge University, where he was elected President of the Union, Pav has been appointed an employment tribunals' member and a Public Appointments Ambassador to promote race, gender and disability equality in public life. He was an elected a councillor in the London Borough of Lambeth where he chaired the Children and Young People's Service. Pav has also served as an LGBT equality advisor to Ken Livingstone, the former Mayor of London, and remains a Director of UK Black Pride.

Pav won a Gold Medal at the British Diversity Awards in 2000; Ethnic Student of the Year in 2001; was a top 50 entrant in the Pink List 2007; received Trinity College Dublin's Award for Outstanding Contribution to Human Rights in 2011; was nominated for a Prime Minister's Big Society Award in 2012 and is shortlisted for a Microsoft National Diversity Award in 2013.

Siani

Siani is happily married with an ever-expanding family of cats, geckoes, and soon-to-be babies! She works with children with SEN both within a special school and for a national children's charity. Siani also loves working on her allotment, baking, and being creative, and has her own small craft business upcycling vintage papers into flowers, gift boxes and more. She works with Worcester Music Festival as a promoter coordinator to raise money for local charities.

www.facebook.com/AnnataTesoro

www.twitter.com/AnnataTesoro

Whilst everyone was invited to contribute a biography, not everyone wanted to.